14.99

D0542721

70°S

0°

80°S

85°S

ANTARCTICA

South Pole

90°E

Beardmore Gl.

a

A n t a r c t i c   M o u n t a i n s

×Pick-up

Ross
Ice Shelf

Mt Erebus
Ross I.

Scott Base
(N.Z.)

ROSS SEA

180°

SHADOWS ON
THE WASTELAND

'How far back do you think
you dropped your wallet?'

by Matt, from the *Daily Telegraph*

To Thea,
Callan and Tarn

SHADOWS
on the
WASTELAND

Mike Stroud

JONATHAN CAPE
LONDON

First published 1993

1 3 5 7 9 10 8 6 4 2

© Mike Stroud 1993

Mike Stroud has asserted his right
under the Copyright, Designs and Patents Act, 1988
to be identified as the author of this work

The lines from T. S. Eliot's *The Waste Land*
which is included in his *Collected Poems 1909-1965*,
are quoted with the kind permission of the
publishers Faber & Faber

First published in the United Kingdom in 1993 by
Jonathan Cape
Random House, 20 Vauxhall Bridge Road, London SW1V 2SA

Reprinted 1993

Random House Australia (Pty) Limited
20 Alfred Street, Milsons Point, Sydney,
New South Wales 2061, Australia

Random House New Zealand Limited
18 Poland Road, Glenfield,
Auckland 10, New Zealand

Random House South Africa (Pty) Limited
PO Box 337, Bergvlei, South Africa

Random House UK Limited Reg. No. 954009

A CIP catalogue record for this book
is available from the British Library

ISBN 0-224-03846-x

Printed in Great Britain by
Clays Ltd, St Ives PLC

Contents

Illustrations

With the exception of number 27, taken by Roger Mear, all the photographs are by Sir Ranulph Fiennes, Mike Stroud and Morag Howell.

Who is the third who walks always beside you?
When I count, there are only you and I together
But when I look ahead up the white road
There is always another one walking beside you

T.S. Eliot
The Waste Land

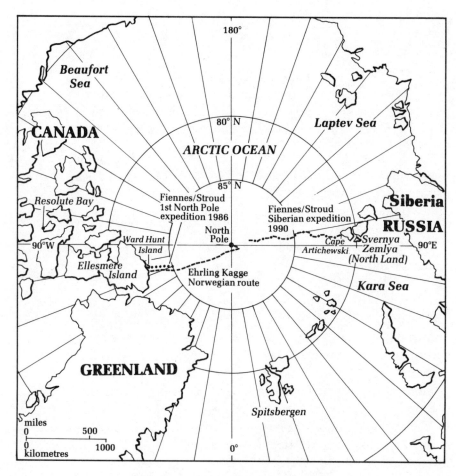

The Arctic: Fiennes/Stroud and the Kagge
attempts to reach the North Pole in 1990

Introduction

I LET THE PHONE ring twice. Just once would have seemed too enthusiastic. It would have revealed that I had been waiting by it, which of course I had. Since earlier in the day, when Roger rang, I had been thinking of nothing else. I knew it would be Sir Ranulph Fiennes, and I knew roughly what he was going to say.

'Is that Mike Stroud? Over.' His voice came through a hiss of static.

'Yes ... yes it is. Er ... hello.'

It was a very bad line and his 'over' had thrown me. Of course it wasn't a line at all but a radio telephone link. Roger had warned me that's what it would be but I hadn't really grasped the implications. Sir Ranulph was far away, on Ellesmere Island, up in the far north of Canada. He was right on the shore of the Arctic Ocean and waiting to set off for the North Pole.

'You know why I'm calling? ... Over.' The voice was firm and he spoke clearly, but there was no pomp. I had assumed it would be plummy.

'Yes ... yes, I do. Roger Mear told me, but I don't know any of the details.'

There was a moment's silence. I hadn't said 'over'. Then he took it up anyway.

'Well, I can't tell you everything. It would take too long over the radio. I want to make an unsupported attempt to reach the North Pole, and I am looking for someone to join me. Will you come out? ... Over.'

Roger had told me that much. Sir Ranulph had called him

I

in the 'Footsteps of Scott' expedition office that morning, and had explained that Oliver Shepard, who had been with him on his Transglobe expedition and who was due to set off for the North Pole with him, had suddenly been called back to Britain. Now he was looking for someone else to join him. Someone who had enough experience not to get hurt in the extreme cold, and who had spent some time manhauling sledges. He had been wondering if any of them – the three who had just walked to the South Pole on the 'Footsteps' expedition – would be interested. Roger considered it, but was committed to writing a book, and Robert Swan and Gareth Wood were unavailable. I had just spent a year with them down in Antarctica as their base doctor, and had been out sledging several times with Roger. He recommended me.

'What would I need to bring with me?' I asked. 'I had to leave a lot of my kit down south after our ship sank. We couldn't get everything out ... Over.'

'Yes, of course. I heard about the ship sinking. I was sorry about that. You'll need everything, but ring my wife, Ginny, and she'll put you on to a chap from Blacks called Alan Day. Ask him for everything you need. We have some stuff up here but it might not fit you, and it might not be what you like. But you have to be fast. It's getting late in the season, and to avoid getting caught by the break-up of the pack-ice, we should have been out there already. Ginny can fix up the air tickets and anything else you need. If she can do it, would you be able to make it on to Monday's flight to Montreal? ... Over.'

My mind raced.

God ... Monday! That's very close. It's Wednesday evening now and I promised to be in Amsterdam on Friday to meet Thea when she arrives home from Australia. What will she think? First I go away for a year to Antarctica, and when she comes out to meet me, the ship sinks. Then because of different ticketing we can't come home together. Now, just as she arrives back, expecting me to stay with her and her family in Holland, I have to tell her that I'm off again. I must at least meet her to explain. It's impossible – or is it? Get the clothing tomorrow morning, go to Amsterdam in the evening. Meet Thea

2

Friday, back Saturday. Pack Sunday, and I am ready. After not getting the opportunity to go to the South Pole this is too good to miss. Thea will understand.

'Okay,' I said. 'I'll be there. How can I contact Ginny? Over.'

He gave me a few more details and the call was finished. For a while I sat there, too stunned to move. What had I committed myself to? Was I mad? I hadn't even met the man, and although I had heard much of his exploits everything that I'd heard wasn't favourable. He was meant to be a tough task master. A rigid military sort of person, reflecting his earlier career and background. Could we get on? The expeditions I had been on were a far cry from the army type.

The next few days were frantic. Into London – choose the gear. No boots – ring the importers. No decent sleeping bag in stock – Ginny had one. Flight to Amsterdam full – take the bus. Meet Thea – upset, but wonderful. Back in the bus – boots not arrived. Fetch them from Yorkshire – out to the airport, and off.

On the plane I had more time to think. The North Pole was only five hundred miles from Sir Ranulph's base camp, and it was flat all the way. Yes, it was across the frozen Arctic Ocean, but surely it would be easier than the Antarctic, where my companions had just walked eight hundred and eighty miles from Scott's Base on the Ross Sea to the South Pole. They had had to climb ten thousand feet through the mountains, moving along crevassed glaciers. I opened Ranulph Fiennes' book about the Transglobe expedition. On that three-year epic, he and a companion, Charlie Burton, had circumnavigated the earth on a vertical axis. Travelling along the Greenwich meridian, they had crossed both the Antarctic, where Oliver Shepard had been with them, and the Arctic, becoming the first men to travel to both Poles. Reading the Arctic section, I began to realise what a nightmare it was to travel on the frozen ocean, an ever-shifting maze of broken ice, pressure ridges and open water. You could fall in, lose your sledges, get crushed by moving ice blocks, and have cracks open under your tent. And there were Polar bears! Everyone had to carry a gun, and I had never even touched one. By the end of the flight I was, frankly, terrified.

Then there was the man himself. The book confirmed my worst fears. He was too hard, too strong, too military for me. He would be horrified when he saw me. No doubt he was expecting someone as big as himself, while I am a very small man. I didn't look forward with relish to either the meeting or the journey.

After a night in Montreal, I took the plane to Resolute Bay – an Innuit village in the far north. Fiennes had told me that I would be met there by a Central Television film crew. Since they would like to get footage of me leaving the aircraft, he wanted me to ignore them and walk straight past the camera, behaving naturally. I duly did as I was instructed, but they ignored me. The film crew couldn't believe that the little man in the blue, puffy duvet jacket was really a Polar explorer. They shot no film and waited for a more realistic sledge-hauler. In the end the director, Paul Cleary, went on to the aircraft to see if I had remained behind. Finally he came into the terminal and, after glancing round, approached me.

'Mike Stroud?' he asked tentatively. Even with no one else there, he clearly found it difficult to imagine that I was the man he sought. Did I really appear so puny as to make it inconceivable that I was proposing to make this journey? If that was his reaction, what would Sir Ranulph's be?

'That's me,' I replied.

'I'm Paul,' he said. 'Welcome to the Canadian Arctic.'

On the next morning, we flew up from Resolute Bay to the most northern point of Canada, Ward Hunt Island. The little Twin Otter landed on a small ice runway outside the base camp huts. I looked anxiously out of the iced-up windows. Three men approached. I knew who they were from Paul's description. Sir Ranulph Fiennes was the tall, dark, lean man, who somehow exuded authority through masking layers of clothing. He came forward quickly, apparently keen to meet his new associate. Oliver Shepard was a little shorter, but nevertheless big and stocky. Unlike Ran, he was clean shaven. I had heard he was a precise and tidy man. He was probably much better suited to Ran than I. The third would be Lawrence Howell, the radio operator. Even he was big. There was no one around to ease the contrast. I felt as if I was a boy among men.

4

I climbed out sheepishly. Sir Ranulph stepped forward and shook hands. He smiled a lot, and welcomed me effusively – all caught on film by the TV crew – but he couldn't hide his disappointment. It was in his eyes. They had registered dismay as soon as I had stepped down from the aircraft. Back in Resolute the evening before, the film crew had told me that Fiennes' idea was to get a brute of a companion, a man who could unthinkingly pull huge loads over the pressure ice obstacles. This brute had already earned the nickname of 'Babe the Blue Ox', after an American cartoon character. They also told me that Fiennes could be difficult. He was fixed in his ways, military minded, didn't take kindly to criticism, and was always the 'leader'. For me it sounded worse by the minute. I was none of these things and had never been the type to acknowledge a leader. To my way of thinking, even though I obviously had much to learn up here, we would be making the trip as equals. Surely two people is too small a number for leadership, and as for Babe the Blue Ox, I am no Ox of any complexion.

We set off two days later – two days in which my opinion changed. Ran wasn't the rigid, thinking military ogre of my expectations. Instead he seemed warm, humorous and easy going. This Baronet – probably the world's greatest living explorer – accepted me as an equal and listened as well as talked. He was anxious to hear about the changes in diet that I wanted to suggest, and he was keen to learn from my experience down South. Wherever he could, he would assimilate the modifications I made in his plan. There was no patronising behaviour of any kind, and I was impressed by the simplicity of the man. Frankly, I was charmed by him.

ONE

★

The Pack

BREAKFAST, a small mug of porridge, was meagre by any standards. Ridiculous for men working as hard as we were. We consumed it before it had time to thicken, our hunger overwhelming our patience. We ate without a word, a continuation of the near silence we had maintained since waking – not due to any ill feeling but because of the prospect of the day ahead. The spirit was crushed by a looming black shadow that would never be dispersed by the feeble Arctic sun.

With the porridge finished, we continued our preparations, difficult when we had been hoping for success, and almost impossible now. Yet neither of us wished to state the obvious, to be the cause of pulling out. It was pitiful. While Ran searched for items by touch, I tried to complete my dressing with fingers that were blistered, raw and stiff. Frostbite numbs only when deep enough to kill the tissues. More superficial damage is exquisitely tender, and it is only with burning needles in the fingertips that one appreciates the force required to pull on thick socks.

From time to time our hands strayed without thinking, popping squares of chocolate into our mouths. We sucked them for a moment, resolved to make them last, but soon chewed and consumed them with urgency. This was followed by an immediate sense of guilt, but we were starving and had lost all self-control. Our ration of two bars was gone before we knew it and nothing was left to fuel the long day. It was incredibly stupid but very human.

Once dressed, Ran left the tent and for a few moments I stopped everything. Unseen, I could relax and pretend for

6

a minute that I didn't have to follow. I thought of home. What had Thea really felt about my going away again? This was the fourth time I'd gone chasing off with the tall man to reach some God forsaken spot that wasn't even on dry land, and to do it by some idiotic self-imposed rules that said we were not to be helped on our way. And all because, though others had tried, no one else had yet succeeded in doing it in a like manner. I knew Thea didn't really think like that – she had been with me in the Antarctic when our ship had sunk – but I couldn't stop the guilt from overwhelming me at times now that we had a family. I pushed the feeling away with the argument that Thea would never have married me if she didn't understand my irresistible urges to disappear from time to time into the wilderness. Would she be giving Callan his breakfast at this moment? Or would she leave that to Sandra who was staying with her during the last weeks of her pregnancy? The baby had been due a week ago – had it arrived? Was it a boy or a girl? I needed to know but there was no way of having my questions answered. We had ditched the radio two weeks ago and could get no news. The backpack had become so painful that I had had to turf out the heavy radio. Would Thea ever forgive me? Was she all right...?

I heard Ran cough impatiently. He had finished the packing and was waiting to take down the tent. By now the cold had seeped through his clothing, chilling his body core and hurting his hands and feet. I swept the hoar frost from walls and roof and joined him outside. We completed the preparations and were ready. I hated this place, I hated Ran, and I hated myself.

We tried to set off quickly in order to warm up, but we couldn't push chilled muscles. It wasn't just the cold that impaired them; we had eaten nowhere near enough to allow them to recover from the previous day's exertion. To operate fully, muscles require a rich supply of glucose from the store within them, and given our poor level of intake, this was depleted from the outset. As a result, glucose manufactured from other tissues of the body had to be drawn in through the blood and each day we were literally consuming ourselves. Our legs felt as if they had just completed a marathon.

Although the realisation had been slow to dawn, we both knew that the end was imminent. We had been in decline for weeks and only the perseverance of the other kept us going. Staggering across the endless sea-ice, driven by a desperation not to give up so close to our goal, we were the embodiment of frailty. I was weakened by 450 miles of wading through knee-deep snow, following the breakage of my ski-binding in the first week, and Ran was in great pain from a deep blister, turned ulcer, that was eroding his heel. For a couple of weeks he had also been losing his vision and now he was nearly blind. He stumbled after my vague outline, cursing as he tripped over every unseen obstacle.

For the moment, however, all our problems were overshadowed by the pain in our near frozen fingers. This happened every morning as packing needed some dexterity. You simply couldn't do up straps wearing inner gloves and two pairs of mitts. Strangely, the fingers were now numb as well as painful. With sensation lost from the bloodless skin, the pain arose from joints and tendons within. Hands curled up inside the mitts felt totally alien, as if frozen sausages had been left in the glove. It would be half an hour before they thawed. Then they would burn fiercely as the blood returned, and new blisters would form where the tissues had turned to ice.

A north-westerly wind of perhaps 30 knots and minus 20°C was blowing on to my left cheek. It iced my goggles almost immediately and soon I too had difficulty in seeing. Ahead, the ground – if that's a fair term for frozen sea water – was a mass of pressure ridges and tumbled ice blocks half covered in snow, flat areas of gleaming new but fragile ice and some older snow-covered floes across which the sledges would pull as if on cement. It made me long for the pulling of Antarctica, the pulling I had experienced with Roger Mear on the 'Footsteps' expedition.

Cracks criss-crossed our path, emanating an evil, dark, frost smoke that blew away to mix with the wind-driven spindrift. Some of the cracks were opening while others were grinding closed and thick sheets of ice were rafting into pressure walls. Despite it being only 22nd April, the spring break-up was progressing in earnest. I cursed it. The whole winter had been warm by Arctic standards, and from the very outset of our journey 48 days before, open water had created dangers and delays. It wasn't fair that such bad luck should have been heaped upon our other misfortunes.

We had set out from Cape Arctichewski, a desolate spot, at the tip of a narrow archipelago that runs north from Siberia, a finger of land pointing towards the Pole. Ran and I, accompanied by some Russian helpers and our radio operators, Flo and Morag Howell, had descended from the big Aeroflot helicopter and readied the sledges. Then, after brief goodbyes from Flo and Mo and some photographs, we were off, bathed in a surreal red light. The Russians had waved smoke flares to wish us well and to ward off the dangers that lay ahead. I touched the flare in my pocket. It was a more specific means of defence against the attentions of a Polar bear and, feeling my gut fear of these animals rise again, I re-checked the position of the revolver – as accessible as possible, in the front of my sledge.

The helicopter took off behind us and then flew low along our path. It wheeled in tribute overhead and we could see small figures waving through the windows. Then it turned and headed south for our base camp – the camp where Flo and Mo would maintain their twenty-four hour watch. They would put a rescue into operation should we need it, and would speak to us briefly by radio every evening. For them it would be a long and patient vigil.

As the thrup of the helicopter receded, Ran led the way across the mile or two of fast ice that clung to the coast, and slowly we approached the tidal shore lead that we had seen as we flew in. This separated us from the freely floating pack and in early March it should have been frozen. Now, however, it was a wide expanse of open water and we realised as soon as we saw it that our chances of reaching our goal were diminished. Clearly the greenhouse effect did not spare the far north of the planet.

The sun's light slowly died, and the rosy hues that had surrounded us changed to silver under a near full moon, although darkness lay in the depths that barred our northward path. The water stretched away to east and west, but directly

9

ahead we could discern a narrow isthmus of thin grey ice that extended to the far side. Across this lay a quick but dangerous path to the relative safety of the thick white ice beyond. That was the true pack, stretching away to the horizon. Glancing at one another, but without the need for verbal confirmation, we changed our plan. Instead of camping at the edge of the tidal lead until daylight, we would set off across the tenuous causeway. If we didn't take advantage of the good weather and the blessing of the bright moonlight, the route might well have broken up by morning.

The ice was extremely thin. A sharp punch from a ski-stick penetrated to a spurt of dark water and, at its narrowest point, our bridge was only twenty yards wide. As we walked the ice flexed in rhythm with our footsteps and gleaming brine lapped over the edges. Open cracks constantly impeded us and it was strange to think, as one spanned these fissures, that the water beneath was already hundreds of feet deep. Stranger still was the fact that, not far ahead, the apparently more solid terrain was a mere skin on an ocean more than ten thousand feet deep. Our whole journey would be on this skin. Our destination was a desolate location in the middle of the Arctic ocean.

We hoped to reach the North Pole with only the supplies and equipment that we dragged behind us – 285lbs each of food, fuel and equipment. Perhaps the task would be impossible, for nowhere on the globe is more inaccessible. Surrounded by millions of square miles of ice, the difficulties surpass those of the hardest mountain peaks – crevasses matched by cracks and open water; rock walls by pressure ridges; and altitude by the terrible Arctic cold. There is also the scale of the journey. In our case, 600 miles lay ahead.

Of course, other expeditions had reached the North Pole, but these had been 'supported', relying on the help of other men, animals or machines for the resupply of necessary provisions. As a result, their sledge weights had been manageable, damaged equipment had been replaced as necessary and – most important – the men had eaten well. Our situation was very different. We planned to receive no outside help and no replacements of any kind. We could eat little, waste no fuel, and break nothing.

All previous unsupported attempts on the North Pole had failed – heavy sledge loads combining with the disrupted ice to defeat the most determined efforts. We knew, for among these failures had been three attempts of our own, including my first journey with Ran. My God, that journey had been awful! We had dragged sledges of nearly 400lbs – even more than on this trip – and it had been so bitterly cold. That was the trouble with Arctic journeys. If you are going to cross a frozen sea, you have to do it in winter, or at least early spring. The temperatures are below minus forty and when it is that cold, you get no ice melt under the runners and the sledge is hard to pull. With no fuel to spare you can't even heat the tent, and that is really miserable.

On that first trip Ran had been in the water early on. On just the third day out of Canada, descending from a pressure ridge, his sledge had broken through thin ice and taken him in with it. He had disappeared for a few seconds, and I thought I had lost him, but then he had popped up and struggled out, shivering as he shook the water off. It was at that moment that I saw his toughness for myself. He made no comment about falling through, or about being cold. He just said, 'Let's get out of here. We need to find a place to camp and wring out my clothing.' It had been unsafe to stop where we were; the ice was too thin and unstable, moving, cracking and grinding. There was no possibility of stopping immediately and it was over forty minutes before we came to a safe floe. By the time we had put up shelter, lit the stove, and were ready to remove his boots, they were frozen on. We had needed to set about them with a knife, and inside there were chalky-white areas to confirm our fears. His foot was badly frostbitten. Even then Ran had no thought of pulling out. He had just asked me to treat it as best I could. The little toe on his right foot, and the area of skin adjacent to it, had been deeply frozen, and a couple of weeks later part of the toe had come off in his sock. By that time, we had used up most of our antibiotics in an attempt to prevent infection, and with only a few days' supplies left, we had been forced to call for our aircraft. It turned out to be the right decision. On the day of the pick-up, his whole foot became a cellulitic mess, with a nasty smelling infection spreading up his leg. Without access to the proper treatment promptly, he would have been in great danger of developing septicaemia – poisoning of the blood, a possibly fatal complication.

It seemed then that a trip to either Pole was not for me. I had returned home disappointed, but feeling privileged to have met and travelled with Ran Fiennes. I didn't think I would do so again.

Christ, I wish I hadn't! Why I should have kept coming back for more I don't know. I suppose it was because that first trip set a record for the most northerly point achieved by an unsupported expedition to date. The eight previous expeditions hadn't even managed our 120 miles north of the Canadian coast, and since it had taken us only seventeen days, it made us think that an unsupported journey to the North Pole was feasible. Even two more failures on the Canadian side with warm weather, thigh-deep snow and broken pack-ice didn't deter us. We just convinced ourselves that we had been unlucky. It was our natural optimism showing through.

We had hoped to do better from Siberia, despite it being more than a hundred miles further to the Pole than from the Canadian side. The ice of the Arctic Ocean is not static but moves around under the influence of winds and ocean currents. On the Canadian side, these cause a slow drift from the Pole southwards and the ice ends up impacting on the coast, exacerbating the pressure between drifting floes. That was why the first fifty or a hundred miles of all our previous attempts had been so packed with pressure ridges. In contrast, we were told that on the Soviet side the ice we crossed would be drifting northwards. There would be fewer local pressure effects and we would benefit directly from the movement. It should aid us by about one and a half miles a day, and so, on a journey of forty-five days, we could anticipate something like sixty or seventy miles of free movement.

The Russian approach would be no gift. Although we were the first foreign expedition to take advantage of glasnost and perestroika, two previous unsupported attempts by the Russian Special Forces had failed. One was abandoned after the early death of one of the team members from uncertain causes;

the other, although reaching the Pole in sixty days, received considerable support by default. There had been another death, and when the body was flown out, two other team members had withdrawn. A further two were then evacuated later in the journey having apparently gone insane. All in all, the men who eventually reached the Pole had ended up getting considerable support from those who had shared their loads for some of the distance but not made it. Although their leader, Colonel Chukov, had at first claimed success, he withdrew his claim when this principle was pointed out to him. He then vowed to try again, and indeed he and his team were to set out a few days behind us.

They weren't our only rivals. On the other side of the Arctic, a three-man Canadian group had left five days prior to us and a three-man Norwegian expedition on the day before. Our journey had both natural obstacles and inter-national competition, with the Norwegians as our greatest rivals. Led by Ehrling Kagge, they were young, strong and determined. Only their lack of experience in the pack would count against them, a lack that would make them slower and more prone to an accident.

Once the thin ice corridor had been crossed safely and we were on the more stable pack, we pitched camp. It was around midnight and we were pleased with our progress. The thin ice had been flat and bare of snow, making pulling our sledges relatively easy. Past experience told us that subsequent days would be harder. They might be less dangerous, but the older, rougher ice would provide a savage mental and physical endurance test.

Our memories had served us well. By Day 2 we were in bad pressure, and although not generally as dense as on the Canadian side, in places it was of equal size and difficulty. In addition, deep soft snow – the consequence of another relatively warm winter – covered everything. We floundered through huge drifts and fell into hidden cracks with dismaying frequency. Crossing this frozen obstacle course was a night-mare. It was also made worse for me by my inability to keep up with Ran, who was so much bigger and heavier. Falling behind, I became increasingly depressed, sinking into black negative moods in which I would contemplate my options for stopping the expedition. In contrast, Ran displayed no hint of weakness. Indeed, his determination seemed endless. He was relentless in pushing on as quickly as possible.

After a week, the pressure began to ease and progress looked promising. Ten-hour days had succeeded in taking us 56 miles at an average of 8 miles per day. This compared well with the four to five miles per day at the start of our previous attempts. My spirits began to rise, but one thing puzzled us. Our combined distance for Days 6 and 7 was only ten miles despite these being the easiest going. Could it be that so near the coast the northerly current was less strong and the untypical northerly winds were causing southward drift?

It seemed to matter little. Our sledges would get lighter, we would grow fitter, and the terrain was already improving. By Day 7 the ice was flat enough to try pulling on skis, which was highly successful. The problems of sinking into soft snow or falling into hidden cracks were greatly lessened, and we speeded up. Then, on Day 8, disaster struck. A half-inch-thick alloy pin, the very basis of the hinge on my right ski-binding, sheared near one end, speckled carbon-coated bubbles within revealing a faulty casting. I was devastated. I had not even dreamed of including this piece of hardened alloy in my list of breakable items and although in retrospect it is easy to say that I should have had a complete spare binding, our sledge weights had exceeded the limit we believed it was possible to pull. When every extra pound meant less fuel or food, hard choices had been inevitable.

Matters were made worse because, being small, I had chosen to wear plastic boots with a rigid sole. These allowed me to kick in with my toes, get my nose right down close to the ice and pull hard over obstacles from an almost horizontal position. Such boots, however, are relatively cold and Ran, with a tendency to get cold feet, had opted to wear soft warmer boots which required a completely different binding. Unable to share my handicap, I was condemned to wade after him. Another 540 miles on foot was a daunting prospect.

Still, working for more than ten hours at a stretch, with no breaks at all, we made reasonable progress. We even travelled when winds reached 60 knots, stumbling through the white-outs, cursing the ice crystals that filled our hoods and stung our eyes like enraged insects. Visibility was frequently down to a couple of yards, footsteps were blown away before the next could be made and shouts buried in white noise. Once separated, we would never have found each other again, and with only one tent, this would have been fatal. Under these conditions we travelled feet apart.

Then, after two weeks, the weather improved and things began to ease for me. I found myself getting stronger and faster as I benefited from the training effect of the pulling while Ran, not as young as he once was and in pain from a deep blister over one heel, became relatively slower. My black moods began to lift and I became optimistic about our chances of success. But the winds had opened up more leads and each cost us precious time while we lashed our sledges into a twin-hulled raft. We always made up the hours we lost on these water crossings, though the resulting thirteen or fourteen-hour shifts took a terrible toll. We both lost weight rapidly despite consuming more than 5,000 calories daily. Steadily we became more fatigued and vulnerable.

The open water problems were also compounded by temperatures rising into the minus twenties. One might easily imagine that this was welcome, but although more comfortable, it led to fresh soft snow further hindering my booted progress. Newly open water also refroze as a soft rubbery mush that could neither be boated on nor walked over and long diversions ate into our schedule. With time against us, we risked crossing ice that normally we would have avoided and, on several occasions, one or other of us fell through. Without each other's help we would have perished and, as it was, each occasion cost us valuable fuel and time.

An even greater problem than either the deep snow or open leads of water was the direction of the prevailing winds. From the moment of our departure, they blew largely from the north, a direction quite contrary to our expectations. Instead of our anticipated free northerly movement, we were constantly blown southwards. By Day 30 we had accumulated some fifteen miles of backward drift. This, combined with the loss of our anticipated forty-five miles forwards, put us sixty miles down. Each night, as we fell into our shivering sleep, we knew that when we awoke, we would have moved back through some of our hard-earned miles.

Of course our logistics left no room for such delays. We had planned on a fast, forty-five day journey to the Pole and had cut weight to the bare minimum. Clearly we now needed to increase our speed, and the only way to do that was to abandon the sledges in favour of backpacks, but by so doing, we would lose the capacity to cross open leads and would have to abandon several items of equipment. Ran insisted that this should include the radio, refusing to carry any part of it, but with Thea expecting the baby within a few days, I could not bear the thought of going out of contact. After sharing out the loads, I added the twenty-six pounds of set, battery and antenna to my sack.

I was in no fit state to carry it. Even Ran found his sack so heavy that, if he fell with skis on, he couldn't get to his feet again without aid. He was like a beetle stranded upside down. Without skis, I could get to my feet alone, but it wasn't all that helpful since I could barely walk. The sack weighed nearly a hundred pounds and it ripped my shoulders, strained my neck and crushed my spine. After only three days, my resolve weakened. I abandoned our transmitter/receiver despite a wave of guilt that was made worse by my being unable to get through to our radio operators to explain. Neither they nor Thea could know that the pain had left me with no choice.

After leaving the sledges, progress improved despite the odds. The drift remained against us, the snow deep, and we had further delays from falls into the water, each requiring a tent stop to partially dry our clothing. But the miles passed and slowly our latitude increased. Then, at around 88° north, and really quite suddenly, our strength disappeared – our weight losses had finally reached the point of bodily collapse. Despite rucksacks that now weighed less than fifty pounds, we could only move slowly, and sleep, always difficult on ice that ground and shrieked like a railway goods yard, became impossible on our thinly padded bones. Cold pervaded to the very core of our bodies, and both of us were developing swollen legs, a sure sign of severe malnourishment.

Ran had also developed trouble with his eyes and it was now becoming serious. At the time I didn't know exactly what was wrong. Later, when he was examined by a specialist in London, we learned that he had retinal damage from years of exposure to the high intensity blue light of the Polar regions. He was warned that he should avoid any future exposure or take great care in his selection of goggles and sunglasses – most of which are not designed to cut out the blue end of the spectrum. Whatever the cause, it was clear that he was in danger of losing his sight permanently and I suggested we should stop. But Ran knew that every mile travelled raised thousands of pounds more for the Multiple Sclerosis Society and he seemed fired by this thought. He calmly talked of the possibility of a future life of touch, smell and sound, while at the same time trying countless arrangements of face mask, goggles and sunglasses. Each was foiled by the icing of the lenses.

Eventually, on Day 44, our daily distances began to decrease and I had the first attack of hypoglycaemia. After a delay with open water, we had tried to walk through the night, but before long I started feeling strange and dropped back. We had to stop for Ran to give me sweetened tea. My brain was running short of glucose fuel as my body tried to answer the unreasonable demands I was putting on my muscles. We had almost reached the end of the road, and with only two more degrees to cover, the hope of stringing out our rations to allow us to walk the last few miles was both unrealistic and dangerous. We decided to eat a little more and to go on until we had two full days' food left, just enough to cover us while waiting for a pick-up.

During the last week I was always out ahead. Ran's deteriorating sight prevented him from adhering to his previous practice of always being in front. For years he had been leading expeditions: he hated to follow, hated to show any sign of physical weakness, but there was nothing he could do about it. Meanwhile I was enjoying myself. It gave me something to think about. Time went by a little faster if you had to plan the route through the obstacles. The secret was to pick the compromise between due north and the most favourable terrain. The pressure ridges caused most delays and were best avoided, but they had to be crossed somewhere and long distances east or west were wasteful. It was a question of how far one should be diverted to find an easy crossing point. Deep snow was also slow and there the disadvantage of having no skis was greatest. Best of course was the new ice, where I gained some respite by walking over a smooth firm surface, though always at the risk of falling through. Only experience, earned the hard way, could help our judgement. But today something was wrong. I was crossing a ploughed field. Mud was sticking to my feet and making them as heavy as lead. My mind was leaving the Arctic Ocean.

The restaurant wasn't far now. Just beyond the wood and into the town. I would have a hamburger. No, a cheeseburger, with large fries and a chocolate milkshake. Perhaps Thea would be there too. With Callan, although he might not like the food.

Then I was there – but it wasn't the same restaurant, or for that matter the same town. It was a Sunday in a country hotel. Starter, roast beef and yorkshire pudding, my father's treat following the successful expedition. As I was about to start, there was crying from the carry cot. Our new baby. Boy or girl? I got up to take a look but someone was calling my name from elsewhere in the room. Who was it? Why was my father pushing me? No – not my father. Ran was shaking me by the shoulder. Why Ran?

'Mike, are you all right?'

'Off courshe, I jusht wanted to shee the baby.'

'Mike, unless the wind has changed you are off course, it's blowing over my left shoulder.'

I checked the compass. Near south – entirely the wrong direction. Stupid of me, just losing concentration. But why couldn't I see properly, and why were my legs like jelly?

'Shorry, I wassh dray deaming.'

The words were slurred and inarticulate. Ran knew what it meant. He put down his pack and started unpacking the tent. As he said later, it was like the drunk leading the blind, and he realised that it was far too dangerous to go on. For me that realisation came more slowly. It required hot sweet tea and some of the next day's chocolate to give my brain the sugar that it needed to function. I had been hypoglycaemic again, and for the sake of safety, now was the time to call for removal with the satellite beacon. Our attempt on the North Pole was over after covering more than 500 miles of the 600-mile journey.

TWO

★

A Change of Direction

EHRLING KAGGE sat down to enthusiastic applause. His presentation had been fine. As good as mine and yet he had spoken in a language foreign to him – clear, precise, and amusing. He had also managed to state his case, that when he and his partner, Borg Ousland, reached the North Pole three weeks after we withdrew, they had done so unsupported. In his opinion, the injury and evacuation of the third member of their team on Day 10 was irrelevant.

Now it was my turn again. Time to make a fool of myself? Quite possibly. Reluctantly I got to my feet and the audience became quiet. Some of them must have wondered what I was going to say. Others must have guessed.

'Ladies and gentlemen. Many of you will have heard that Ran Fiennes and I don't fully agree with Ehrling's interpretation of his journey. I want to take this opportunity to try and clarify the points that we've been making. Certainly I wish to put straight the misreporting that has occurred.'

Muttering and murmuring came from various parts of the room. To my right, a small group jeered. The Royal Geographic Society was not used to dissension – at least, not since the days of Burton and Speke and their arguments over the source of the Nile. I flinched but carried on.

'One thing we have never said, despite being quoted in the press, is that Ehrling and his companion, Borg Ousland, were cheats. Both Ran and I agree that they made a magnificent journey and, obviously, they honestly believe it was unsupported. However, we think that they have failed to appreciate that they did receive support.'

More murmurings from the audience. There was one call of 'must we listen to this?' But it was not the majority. Most people were quiet and listening intently. I got the impression that I was to be given a fair hearing.

'Ehrling and his two companions set off to walk to the North Pole, as we did, unsupported. But, after ten days, Gier was injured and had to be evacuated. This entailed Ehrling and Borg waiting four days for the plane to arrive and during that time they admit that they consumed Geir's food rather than the supplies they carried themselves. As a result, they benefited in a number of different ways. Firstly, during the earliest, coldest and hardest part of the journey, a third man helped move the general equipment. Secondly, they effectively ate extra food and had a free rest. It may have been after only ten days, but that extra food went into their body stores which would have already been depleted. It helped them later and, in terms of resupply, was just as effective as putting food on their sledges.'

More calls – I heard the word 'rubbish' – but I was concentrating and missed the gist of it.

'Thirdly – the most telling point but the most difficult to express – when they planned their expedition they planned for three men. The limiting factor on any of these trips is the weight one believes one can pull. Within that limit, one takes as many days' food and fuel as possible. Ehrling calculated this to be sixty-five days, but if he had planned for two men in the first place, he would have taken less. When the third member of the team dropped out after ten days, Ehrling and Borg went on with fifty-five days of food. They considered that that was fair enough, but they were fooling themselves. When they reached the Pole with no food, they should have realised that without Geir's help they might never have got there. If we had had that much assistance, we might also have reached that goal.'

More jeers came from a small group on the right, including a sarcastic cry of 'Oh, you poor things.' Although later I wished I had come up with a quick riposte, perhaps something about the meeting not being a football match, it was difficult to think fast enough.

'Finally, many of you will have heard of the Russian,

Colonel Chukov. Last year, he and his men reached the Pole but a number of his party had been forced to drop out. He also claimed, at first, that his journey was unsupported, but when it was pointed out that – for similar reasons to those I have just expressed – he and his companions had received help, he withdrew his claim.'

I paused. There was silence.

'Ladies and gentlemen, if a team climbed Everest without oxygen, except for just a little on the way, their claim would not be accepted. This Norwegian team may well have been successful if the third man had not been injured, but he was, and as a result they were even more unlucky than we were. They completed a magnificent journey, but not an unsupported one. I believe that they are sincere in their interpretation of their trip, but they are wrong. If they are not, Colonel Chukov made the first unsupported journey to the North Pole last year. Thank you.'

There was more applause, not as enthusiastic as greeted either of our main presentations but not hostile either. I hadn't made a fool of myself, and to most people I was just voicing an opinion. They either agreed or disagreed, or perhaps they didn't care anyway.

Kagge stood up again. How detailed was his defence going to be? Certainly he had one powerful argument. Prior to leaving on the expedition he had asked Ran what would happen if one of the team members had to be evacuated. Ran had replied that as long as none of the man's supplies were taken further, he would still consider it as an unsupported trip. If only they had asked me the same question. I had always said to Ran that if I dropped out and he continued, he would be fooling himself if he considered it unsupported. Now Ehrling was in a position to use Ran's statement. He didn't. He just restated that it wasn't support since they had only eaten while waiting. If I disagreed, the answer was simple – I could go back and do it properly. I could not deny it. We shook hands and the audience appreciated the gesture. As gentlemen we had agreed to differ.

The meeting began to break up. People approached me with either general congratulations or specific questions, few

1 Ran in Arctic pack, attempting to reach the North Pole from Siberia in 1990

2 Crossing open water in the Arctic pack

3 A brief stop for soup

4 Walking without skis on soft snow

5 After abandoning the sledges, crossing open cracks became difficult

of them about the unsupported argument. Roger Mear called me a brave man. I thought he was referring to the journey we had made, but he meant my voicing dissent at the RGS. Another polar traveller, Geoff Summers, said simply: 'He's talking rubbish. You don't even need the logical arguments. Unsupported trips just don't involve visits from aircraft.' It was nice to have some backing.

After the meeting I dined with Ehrling Kagge and the RGS President, and continued the debate. It extended to other possible expeditions. Kagge told me that he thought an unsupported Antarctic crossing was possible, but that he was not ready to take it on. He would try it in two to three years' time when he had 'recaptured the hunger'. I tried to keep my expression bland. Ran and I were already making plans for the same journey in 1992/93. The last thing I wanted was a re-run of the race.

After stopping in the Arctic, we had triggered our satellite beacon with the coded message for a pick-up. We found it incredibly annoying that this was later described as a rescue. Such a term invariably leads to comments about irresponsibility and endangering others, and it reinforces the arguments of the 'they're a load of daft buggers' faction. As far as we are concerned, we have never been rescued from anywhere. We have always simply arranged for a chartered aircraft, paid for in advance, to collect us from the farthest point that we could reach.

Waiting in our tent, we hadn't been altogether clear about the details of the removal plan, although we knew that a helicopter would come out from one of the Soviet research bases that drift on the ice floes through the winter and early spring. It seemed likely that we would have a long wait, and would just have to be patient. It was cold in the tent. If you are thin, your metabolism produces less heat and there is little insulation to keep it in. It's also cold if you eat too little. A good meal increases heat production for hours. We had almost nothing left – one day's ration, a couple of soups, and a bottle of fuel. We tried to sleep and failed, so we turned to one of our tent games – twenty questions to guess a character, real or imaginary, living or dead. After many games earlier in the journey, our approaches were quite sophisticated, and weeks in each other's company had attuned our thinking. It was rare for either of us not to manage the correct deduction, even with characters such as Lot's wife and Omar Khayam. Hours passed. We felt close, linked by a camaraderie that had grown through the hardships we had endured, a feeling of unified suffering and achievement, tainted only by our failure. Try as we might to talk up our attainments, we were bitterly disappointed.

Ran heard it first and thought he was hallucinating. We had put out the satellite call only seven hours previously and had anticipated waiting for days. Yet he was right, there was a helicopter not far away. I rushed outside with the flares while Ran scrabbled to trigger the local aircraft beacon. Pulling the tag of the first flare, it ripped off in my hand. So much for the Polar bear deterrent. The second one worked and a huge plume of red smoke surrounded me and the tent. The helicopter turned towards us, the crew probably wondering why I was a coughing, spluttering wreck. I hadn't been able to read the Russian instruction 'STAND BACK – DO NOT HOLD' on the flare. Still, we had been seen and were to be plucked back to civilisation.

It was with us moments later, disgorging a party of Russians who shook our hands, patted our backs and pressed food bags upon us. At the same time, they urged us to get aboard for they had little fuel and were concerned that the weather was going to change. We climbed in, took off and headed east – our destination, a floating camp about 400 miles distant. During the flight, Ran and I enthusiastically investigated the food bags. They contained rusting tins of gristly meat, awash with thick cold gravy, tinned fish that was no better, but no chocolate or sweets, for which we craved. Nevertheless, by the time we reached our destination, there was nothing left.

As the aircraft approached the floating ice camp, we saw immediately that all was not right. The Russians had been trying to tell us something about the early break-up of the ice and now we understood what they had been going on about. Beside the camp, the long ice runway, carefully prepared to allow wheeled jets to land, was broken into several fragments. The Siberian coast was too far away for a helicopter. It seemed that we were to be on the research station for a while. We landed and were ushered into the tent of the Base Commander. He spoke English a little better than his colleagues and explained the situation to us. We would have to wait while a new runway was constructed about 18 miles away, a process that would take about a week. During that time we were his guests, and he would extend all the hospitality he could. However, he hoped that we appreciated that his supplies were never luxurious, and at that moment were low. He also said that in two decades of pack-ice research, he had never experienced a significant break-up before late May – more evidence of man's mark upon the planet.

From the welcome we received, one wouldn't have guessed that supplies were low. The entire camp of about forty men gathered and plied us with caviar, sausage and camp-baked bread. There was also Arctic Char, a salmon-like fish that they pulled from ice holes, allowed to freeze, and then ate raw. Thinly sliced, and accompanied by mayonnaise and apparently unlimited vodka, it was wonderful. We went to sleep late, full, and not a little drunk.

During the next few days, the men constantly came to visit us, bringing with them what food they could – mostly the vile tins of meat and fish, but occasionally more welcome tins of jam, butter or cheese. Ran and I ate constantly, slept frequently and talked endlessly. Soon those defective short-term memories were operating, or at least mine was. Just days after the end of almost unbelievable hardship, we were planning a further attempt on the North Pole. This time, not for Ran and I, but for myself and another partner. Ran would leave it to younger men and would act as Patron. He felt it was time to hang up his boots.

The new runway was complete after six days, and it was with considerable excitement that we waited for the aircraft. Then, during the wait, Ran began to look uncomfortable, with pain developing in his left side and loin. At first I thought it was simple indigestion, but it became more serious, coming in waves which made him sweaty and nauseous. I could hardly believe it. Out in the middle of the Arctic Ocean, Ran was getting renal colic. He clearly had a kidney stone stuck at the top of his ureter – the tube that leads from kidney to bladder – and there was nothing we could do about it but hope it would be passed. Before long, he needed major pain killers, and with our limited supplies, morphine was the answer. The result was that when our journey finally commenced, Ran was sedated and feeling unwell. He could only watch with a mystified expression as, flying back to base camp, I consumed the entire pack of chocolate goodies that had been sent up by Flo and Morag. By the time he came round, in a little less pain, they were all gone.

After our return to Britain, we received a buoyant reception and congratulations from all directions, but for me these were as nothing when compared with seeing my new baby daughter, Tarn. She was gorgeous, and for a time I was the happiest man alive. Then, a couple of weeks later, the two Norwegians reached the Pole, and although we tried to explain the issues as best we could, the public, and even friends, became confused about what we were saying. Everyone seemed to become embarrassed by the whole affair. Whether the Norwegian journey was supported or not was quite unimportant for most people. As a result my interest in heading north again declined and finally disappeared altogether when Ran – who had taken several weeks to become forgetful – hinted at an Antarctic expedition. I was eager to listen.

Ran's Transglobe companions, Oliver Shepard and Charlie Burton, had put forward the idea of making an unsupported crossing of Antarctica via the South Pole – another yet to be achieved 'first'. Ran was keen but wanted me to go along as well. At first Ollie and Charlie expressed reservations about my joining them, for they saw the trip as a kind of 'old boys' reunion. When they examined the practicalities of the idea, they began to see that it could be useful to strengthen the team. Eventually they had to face up to the fact that they themselves could never get into shape for such a journey and concluded that theirs would be an organising role. The expedition itself would be left to Ran and me.

When my family and friends heard that we were thinking of going off again, they simply couldn't understand it. I was constantly pressed with the question: why? Often I was tempted to answer in the words of Wally Herbert, the first man to cross the Arctic Ocean, who said, 'Those who need to ask, will never understand the answer, while others who feel the answer will never need to ask.' But I didn't want to sound too evasive, and so tried to explain the motivation that allowed me to undertake such hardship.

There was the challenge, the sense of satisfaction in taking something on and seeing it through. It is exactly the same as walking up a mountain which in good or bad weather is equally enjoyable. The pleasure is derived from stepping away from normal life and responsibilities and proving something to yourself. You don't worry about the usual things when you climb up a mountain, whether a Himalayan peak or something as straightforward as Snowdon. The Polar regions are merely a bigger step away, a stride so large that you reach another planet. By stepping so far from normal existence, you see your life as a whole in a different perspective.

There was also the scientific side of the journey. My research interests lie in human fitness, nutrition and the control of body weight. In my job at the Army Personnel Research Establishment, I conduct research on the effects of different diets on physical performance and body composition, and am fascinated by the fact that, after decades of international research, no one can tell you why one person is thin and another is fat. The answer must lie in the interaction between diet and exertion, and these expeditions provide unique opportunities to look at that interaction in the extreme. We would lose weight while eating an enormous amount. It would be a strange situation, but one that would yield information that was pertinent to the normal. There is no way in which similar information can be gathered in the laboratory. Nobody is ever going to work that hard for that long just for an experiment.

There was one less acceptable motivation – ego. How much of me wanted to go out and prove myself, not internally, but to others? How much of me wanted to revel in admiration and praise? They were difficult questions and although I liked to think they were unimportant, I sometimes wondered whether I was fooling myself and just not admitting that it was the achievement in the eyes of others that mattered. After all, everything we tried was an attempt to be 'first', and if it had been done before, I doubt that we would have bothered with it. This is a far cry from the urge to follow the tourists up Snowdon, and would seem to hint at a need to impress. On the other hand, it does not altogether exclude self-satisfaction as a motive. Doing something first or best can still be done for oneself.

Two more ingredients are required to permit you to undertake these journeys which, in themselves, can be so arduous. People talk of courage, strength, and determination, but these qualities do not count for as much as an optimistic outlook, and above all a very poor short-term memory. You need to be able to forget the hardships at the end of every day in order to face the next, and then, at the end of the expedition, you need to forget everything but the good times. Only in that way would you ever consider returning for more.

The majority of people on whom I pressed these rationalisations heard me out with a stare of blank incomprehension. Try as I might to explain, many of them would have agreed with a journalist who described us as 'a few stock cubes short of a ration'. In the face of this response, I turned more and more frequently to the easy way out – I was going for charity. Our expedition to the Arctic had raised more than two million pounds for Multiple Sclerosis research, and now we planned to do the same in Antarctica, where we hoped to raise even more. I found it immensely satisfying that we could achieve such benefit from our journeys. I also knew that I would find it helpful when I wanted to give up on the walk. Of course, I would have reckoned on going even if there were no opportunity for fund-raising but nevertheless, as an explanation for the people who could never grasp the attractions of a Polar expedition, the excuse was a God-send. For that kind of money it would be acceptable to stand on your head in a broom cupboard for three months. They had no answer to that.

Early 1991 saw us poring over maps of the Antarctic, wondering if such an outrageous undertaking was at all possible. It certainly would be extremely difficult. Unlike the North Pole, the South Pole lies at the heart of a huge, high altitude, ice desert and at the continent's narrowest point, the coasts on both sides are flanked by huge, floating areas of ice, the Filchner and Ross ice-shelves. Traditionally they have always been considered as an integral part of any southern journey, and crossing them would make the journey more than eighteen hundred miles. But what a journey! It was so simple. We would just set out with all we could pull and with the whole continent ahead of us. It would be an enormous challenge, and one that only men pulling their own sledges could attempt. Everyone assumes that it is possible to go farther with dog teams or motorised vehicles pulling sledges full of fuel. They are quite mistaken. Dogs could never pull loads great enough to see them over anywhere near that distance, unless you have dog eating dog, as Amundsen did. Tracked vehicles, skidoos, whatever forms of motorised transport could never pull their own fuel so far. Only men dragging their loads behind them could possess enough drive and determination to have any chance of success; and although that chance might be small, I was convinced it was there.

Shackleton had first dreamed of crossing Antarctica after the South Pole had been attained by Amundsen and Scott in 1912. His plan was to set off from the South American side of the continent, the Weddell Sea, cross the Filchner ice-shelf to reach the continental coast, and then ascend to the plateau and the South Pole. He would then cross to the far side following the route he pioneered in 1909, and which Scott had used on his South Pole journey. Once he reached the mountains and the Beardmore glacier descent to the ice-shelf on the other side, he would pick up food and fuel depots laid by a separate arm of the expedition, the 'Ross Sea shore party'.' The whole expedition was to prove spectacularly ill-fated. Shackleton, his crossing team, and his ship's crew, found themselves marooned on the Weddell Sea pack-ice after their ship was crushed and sank, while over on the Ross Sea side the shore party watched helplessly as their ship was blown out with nothing but a tiny part of their supplies unloaded.

The resulting tales of hardship beggar belief. Shackleton's team dragged open lifeboats across the pack to the free ice edge, and then sailed or rowed more than a thousand miles to Elephant Island. A smaller group, led by Shackleton himself,

SHADOWS ON THE WASTELAND

then rowed across the horrendous southern ocean to summon help from the whaling stations of South Georgia. It is astonishing that none of these men perished. Meanwhile the Ross Sea shore party had an even harder time. Convinced that Shackleton and his men would be trekking over from the Pole, entirely dependent on picking up their depots, they determined to lay those depots whatever the cost. They therefore spent the winter living off seal meat and scavenging for food from the frozen supplies of earlier expeditions. By doing this, they preserved the sledging rations for the following spring. Then, weakened by a winter of poor nutrition, nine of the ten men set out to manhaul almost four hundred miles across the ice-shelf to lay the depots at the foot of the Beardmore. They did so, and most got back, but the journey cost the lives of three of them, and the sanity of the one who stayed behind.

After this disastrously unlucky expedition, decades passed before there was another attempt at a crossing, this time successful. In 1957 Sir Vivian Fuchs and Sir Edmund Hillary undertook the Trans-Antarctic expedition – Fuchs approaching the Pole from the Weddell Sea, while Hillary approached from the Ross. Both teams used special tractors to haul huge loads of fuel, food and scientific equipment, and aircraft resupplied them on the way. It was a massive exercise, but eventually Fuchs and his group managed to cross the continent successfully, picking up depots on the second half of the journey that Hillary had left for them. It was a triumph of logistics, and not inconsiderable hardship, and an enormous wealth of scientific data was gathered en route.

After that there were a number of other mechanised crossings of various parts of Antarctica, chiefly for scientific purposes, before Ran Fiennes, Charlie Burton and Ollie Shepard, made their 'adventure' Transglobe crossing. They used open skidoos, and once again, aircraft were employed to resupply food fuel and spare equipment. Then, in 1985, the 'Footsteps of Scott' expedition – on which I had been the winter base doctor – signalled a return to travel by older means. Robert Swan, Roger Mear and Gareth Wood manhauled sledges, unsupported, from Scott's hut at Cape Evans by way of Scott's route to the South Pole. They were then flown back to the coast, but they had completed a distance of 883 miles, the longest unsupported journey ever made. They had also given the signal that Antarctica, although difficult to reach, was one of the few regions on Earth that could still offer fundamental physical challenges. All that was needed were men and women who wished to take them up.

Two more Antarctic crossings took place in 1990. Both used old methods of travel, but were resupplied from the air. Will Steiger led a multi-national team that crossed Antarctica with dogs, taking the longest possible route. In seven months of travel, they covered six thousand miles from the tip of the Antarctic peninsular, via the South Pole, to the Soviet station of Mirny. Simultaneously, the world's greatest mountaineer, Reinhold Messner, accompanied by the German Polar explorer, Arved Fuchs, manhauled across the continent at its narrowest point. They were also resupplied by aircraft, both en route to the Pole, and at the Pole itself.

So what did these earlier expeditions tell us of the feasibility of an unsupported crossing. When Robert Swan asked Roger Mear to join him on an expedition to repeat Scott's return journey to the South Pole, Roger had seen a different challenge. He wrote:

> Why not dispense with all the clutter and go alone and unsupported, in one push, with a minimum of food – no depots, no air support, no dogs, no ponies or mechanised vehicles – just two men, hauling sledges on the longest white walk in history? Of course, it could never be a two way journey on foot as Scott's had been, for no one could drag the weight...

This was not encouraging. Not only was our journey of greater length than Scott's return journey would have been, but because it was a crossing, we could not lay any depots on the way out to be picked up on the way back. Messner wrote:

> I had difficulty in pulling the sledge with its initial weight of 80 kilos. I had to strain in my harness like a horse on dry drift snow in order to progress. It didn't feel good.

If 80 kilos didn't 'feel good', what would our proposed loads feel like? We were going to have to set off with more than 200 kilos. Furthermore, Messner had difficulties completing his crossing in one season, despite using aircraft to move his food and fuel, and getting considerable help from the use of wind sails. He also commenced his journey on the true coast of Antarctica rather than at the edge of the ice-shelf, and this saved him nearly two hundred miles compared to the journey we wished to attempt. Although we recognised that his approach would make our chances of success greater, we were traditionalists. After his journey, Messner claimed that he had fulfilled Shackleton's dream. We didn't agree that he had even attempted it, but we wanted to do so. As well as crossing the continental landmass, we would also cross those ice-shelves, but the earlier expeditions gave only one answer – beyond doubt the trip was impossible. It was not the answer that we sought, so we ignored it.

THREE

★

The Pursuit of Knowledge

THE PAIN was terrible, quite unlike anything I had ever experienced. Waves of pain emanated from within my thigh, travelling into my groin and abdomen. I felt sick and broke into a sweat. Was this the 'sensation of pressure' he had mentioned? I should have known one could never trust a doctor. It came again and I grasped the couch and groaned through clenched teeth. I had to keep the leg relaxed but it was impossible with my thigh jerking in convulsive spasm. A biopsy needle – thick as a ball-point pen – followed the scalpel incision and was plunged deep into my muscle. I couldn't imagine how a hospital patient with only the haziest idea of what was being done might respond to this.

The aim of the biopsies was to take small chunks of muscle to be looked at under the microscope and to be checked for chemical content. For the sake of the chemical analyses, it was vital that local anaesthetic didn't contaminate the sample, so only the skin could be anaesthetised and beyond that I just had to accept the pain. Still, it would be worth it. When would anyone have another chance to look at what happens to muscles working hard for three months yet starving. The results should tie in with the other measurements being made today and repeated after the journey and should also correlate with the experiments we were going to make en route. The latter would be the hardest to perform. Cold, hungry and exhausted, it would take considerable self-discipline to maintain records of our weight and food intake, and to collect frequent blood and urine samples. But later, analysis of the samples would allow us to estimate energy expenditure, the turnover of our muscles, and the changes in our blood fats and various

33

hormones. The work should give us an understanding of our physical decline in the face of the overwhelming stress that I knew we would go through.

'Just a few moments more.'

The disembodied voice was lost in another deep, searching surge of agony. Then there was a third, and a fourth, then bliss! It was over. I lay with the bleeding leg limp, completely wrung-out by the experience. It had been so much worse than I had expected. Mind you, at least I was conscious. Sharon and Andrea, two of my staff who had come to witness the ministrations of the Nottingham University team, had both fainted.

It was all for science. The research programme was going well, and now, less than a week from departure, Ran and I were going through our pre-departure tests. It would be worth all the pain, although I must admit that I was already having second thoughts about the post-expedition muscle biopsy. I was planning to do it to myself if necessary, but having experienced it, I wasn't quite so sure. Perhaps if we did make it all the way across, there would be a doctor at the New Zealand or the American Base who might oblige. The more I thought about it, the more essential it became that they did. I would never be able to do that to myself.

Now it was Ran's turn. Christ, what was he going to think of it? He couldn't bear the sight of a small needle, and I had had him pass out on me before over a blood test. Still that was their problem. A problem for the Nottingham KGB, as Ran had christened them.

'Okay Ran, it's all yours.'

He was sitting in the library talking to a reporter from the *Sunday Express*. Maps were laid out on the table where earlier he and I had been plotting our route. It was easier to work out all the compass deviations now, rather than try to do it in the tent. The thought made me cold now that the journey was getting close.

'Lead on,' said Ran nervously, and I took him down to the medical room.

Of course the scientific programme was just one part of the plan that had evolved slowly and fallen into place over the last year and a half. I thought back. We had come a long way since our first look at the maps.

To begin with, it had been necessary to work out how to get there and then to get out again. In 1984, when the Footsteps of Scott expedition was being planned, the only way in which a private group could enter Antarctica was by ship, and as a ship could go in only after the pack-ice had melted, the Footsteps party had been obliged to arrive in the late summer and then over-winter, so as to be ready in the following spring to set off overland and take full advantage of the short Antarctic summer. Since then things have changed. An air charter company, Adventure Network International (ANI), was set up in 1986 specially to take expeditions into the Antarctic, and this has made planning much easier. At the same time, operating a long-distance air service to an icebound wilderness is not inexpensive. For us the cost of flights in both directions would have been prohibitive, so we decided to fly in with ANI to the South American side of Antarctica and then to leave the continent aboard the *Frontier Spirit*, a tourist ship that would be paying a visit to Scott's hut on the New Zealand side at the end of the summer.

Once the mode of transport was settled, the time frame for the journey was virtually dictated. As Adventure Network were unable to deliver us to our starting point before the first week of November 1992 and the ship was to leave the continent on 17th February 1993, we had between 100 and 109 days to complete the overland journey. If we could spin out the rations at the end, we could risk taking food and fuel for only a hundred days.

Only a hundred? There was no 'only' about it! By the most optimistic assessment, that made our sledge weights more than 400lbs each, and now it looked more like 450lbs. Such a weight might be impossible to move. It would certainly make us slow. Both Scott's original journey in 1912 and the Footsteps expedition in 1985/6 had taken 70 days to reach the Pole pulling far less per man than 400lbs. How could we expect to complete the other half of the journey with less than thirty days' food? There was only one solution. When Messner made his crossing in 1990 he had carried and used sails to great effect, particularly on the second half of his journey where Antarctic winds tend to blow away from the Pole. We had to do the same. We had to get enough food and fuel to the Pole as quickly as possible and then use the wind to help us cover the next stage faster. Roger Mear suggested the use of a modified parachute called an 'Up-ski', but Ran would not hear of it. The subject had arisen again on that morning of the biopsies. We were looking at the maps when I mentioned it as a solution to the weight problem.

'Mike, there's no use in you going on about it. I will not sail if I can help it. To me, it is support. It's like saying you're going to row the Atlantic and then hoisting the sheets. To my mind, it's cheating.'

I was exasperated. 'It is not *cheating*,' I said firmly. 'Scott, Shackleton, Amundsen, Messner – they all used sails. It's just taking advantage of nature. Not to use the wind is the artificial restriction. It would be like refusing to use skis. It's like your Atlantic oarsman insisting it only counts if he rows from east to west rather than using the Gulf Stream, and for that matter, the equivalent is an ocean that has never been crossed without using powered ships. A sail is less support than the radio.'

In fact, Ran had been against taking a radio as well – on the grounds of weight. He thought it best to take only a satellite beacon. Still, since that would be used to let people know our position and whether we were all right, it wasn't any different in terms of whether one saw communications as support. I was leaving behind two young children as well as a wife, and had wanted to take a radio in order to be contactable. I would then be able to abandon the expedition if a serious problem arose at home. That difference of opinion was resolved by my refusing to go unless I had my way.

'The radios are entirely different,' Ran said irritably. 'They don't help us physically in any way. They make it safer, but no easier.'

'But even if you don't *like* sails, we can't make it without them,' I responded testily. 'Messner took forty-five days from the Pole to Scott Base, and used sails for more than half of it. There's no way we'll have that much time, even if we get to the Pole quickly. Even with sails, the logistics don't add up!'

36

'Look, Mike, you're not going to persuade me to use them unless it's absolutely necessary. I'll agree to take them, and we can decide after the Pole whether to use them or not. That's as far as I'll go on the subject.'

'Fine,' I said with relief. To myself I murmured, 'If we've got them, we'll use them.' I knew I had won the debate.

Ran came out of the medical room looking pale, grey and sweaty. He had enjoyed it as little as I had, but he had survived. We moved on to the other tests: running on treadmills, measurements of strength, body weight under water; and resting metabolism before and after a test meal. All in all, two days of being the guinea pigs in my own research – a salutary experience.

While the tests were conducted, we went on talking to the reporter from the *Sunday Express* who had promised to cover our fund raising for the Multiple Sclerosis Society along with our scientific experiments. They would even include a box to encourage readers to send donations to the charity.

The main press conference had been held in the previous week, complete with the obligatory publicity stunt. On this occasion it had consisted of jumaring up ropes that were hung from the top of a two-hundred-foot tower block in Battersea. This had proved to be incredibly difficult, and actually served a useful purpose: it emphasised that if we were to go down a crevasse, escaping up the rope with a sledge was going to be almost impossible. It also served to emphasise Ran's fear of heights, which was even greater than that of needles. As we climbed, and the boats on the Thames became smaller and smaller, he had steadfastly refused to look down, horrified by the exposed position in which he found himself. Yet it was a demonstration of the man's determination. He had been the instigator of the performance, even though he was well aware of his fear and knew that he would have to cope with it. Ran has always been prepared to meet his fears face to face.

The meetings with journalists resulted in a mixture of good, bad and cynical articles. One of the reasons for our dissatisfaction with the reporting was the reappearance of Ehrling Kagge. In mid-1992, we had heard that Kagge was also planning an Antarctic expedition, and immediately assumed that it would be in direct competition to our own and that his 'hunger' must have returned faster than anticipated. Our inquiries revealed, however, that the situation was not quite so bad as we'd supposed. Kagge had been planning an unsupported crossing for the following year, and by the time he heard of our plans, he was unable to move his project forward. He then decided that something else had to be done and settled upon an attempt to travel alone to the South Pole at the same time as us. This, the newspapers told us, was another race – a re-run of Scott versus Amundsen – but that was absurd. He was going only halfway, and his loads and speed would not be comparable with ours. Such niceties failed to find expression in reports by a press not known for allowing accuracy to spoil a good story.

Unfortunately Ran made one mistake when talking to the *Express* reporter. As always, he responded to the inevitable question 'why do you do it?' with the simple answer that avoided trying to explain complex motives: he did it as a job because he needed the money. It was a statement guaranteed to irritate me for it destroyed anything of value in the undertaking, and was a snub to the charity that benefited from it. Previously the press had either ignored the remark or had made little of it, but this time we were not so lucky. On the day before our departure the *Sunday Express* ran a big article under the headline 'SIR RANULPH OFF TO CONQUER HIS FINANCES'. It neither described the scientific work in any detail, nor focused on the effort for charity. Instead the feature concentrated entirely on Ran's financial motivations. It didn't even fulfil the promise to give instructions about donations. It was a slap in the face for the Multiple Sclerosis Society, and I felt tarred with this mercenary brush. I had doubts that I wanted to go on an expedition with such a man, although later I came to appreciate that this was his let-out answer. He would rather be seen as a down-to-earth man setting about his job than be painted as the eccentric aristocratic explorer.

The enormity of what I was doing to my family didn't strike home until after we had left Heathrow. Up to then the expedition had remained in my mind as an abstract idea. There were so many reasons why it might never really happen. It was so easy to say yes and live in a world of self-delusion.

There one could plan with excitement yet feel inside that one would never really go away – we would never get a sponsor, the logistics of the expedition would be insurmountable, my work would not allow me to go. One by one, these hurdles had fallen away and my assurances to Thea – 'don't worry, we are only thinking about it' – became increasingly false. She had to begin making real plans. How would she cope with my absence and two young children?

Even as we said goodbye at the airport – with me holding Callan on one side, Tarn on the other, and simultaneously hugging Thea – my going did not seem real. Yes, the tears welled from my eyes and there was a gut-wrenching pain in the parting, but it was only for a few weeks, not long. On the plane, I realised that I was talking about months, more than a third of the next year.

The film on the flight didn't help either. I can't remember the title, but it told the story of a man who had witnessed and then prevented a terrorist attack, inadvertently making his family a target for the terrorists. It was the family part that was so difficult. When it came to his children being threatened, the film seemed to contain a message aimed straight at me. How could I let myself leave my vulnerable children? Would they think of me and love me in my absence? Would I return? That was the first time it occurred to me that I might not come home. I didn't really think of the expedition as dangerous, but the prospect of those crevasse fields was not reassuring.

At least we had Mo with us. With the agreement about taking a radio had come the question of taking an operator. At first, neither Mo nor Flo were keen to get caught up in another expedition, though they agreed to help procure our communications equipment. Then, as they became more involved in the planning, Mo grew increasingly interested in going South. Flo had business commitments that kept him but eventually his wife decided to come if she could, though getting her to Antarctica was not easy. Adventure Network normally charged $20,000 for a return trip. She had not only to get in, but to stay at their base camp for a hundred days or more. It looked for some time as if it would be impossible to finance her, but Mo is nothing if not tenacious. Just a few days before we left she confirmed that she would be coming. She had negotiated a cheap ticket to the Antarctic in return for helping Adventure Network with their communications, and obtained some direct sponsorship from various sources to cover her costs.

The advantages of having Mo in the Antarctic were enormous. Radio communications at either end of the earth can be severely effected by auroral activity which disrupts the ionosphere. Although the ANI staff at the base in Patriot Hills were prepared to handle our radio traffic, they were neither well equipped nor free to listen out at all times. Unlike Mo, they would also be unable to appreciate the situation from calls that invariably would be brief due to our severely limited battery power. Mo, on the other hand, understood exactly what an unsupported expedition entailed and what our aims were. She would be able to take a few words of news and combine it with our position to put together a decent press report. She was going to make our journey safer and at the same time help public relations for both the MS Society and our main sponsor, Pentland.

It took nearly thirty-six hours to reach Punta Arenas in the south of Chile, an historic place in world navigation. Situated on the Magellan Strait, it has been for centuries a stopover for trading ships rounding Cape Horn. In the town square there is a large statue of Magellan himself, cast in bronze and sporting a particularly shiny big toe. 'Rub the toe if you wish to return safely' is the legend. I studiously avoided doing so. I had no wish to return to the place but to leave it, enter Antarctica, and exit on the other side. I was looking forward to seeing the statue of Captain Scott in Christchurch, New Zealand, at the end of our journey.

We planned to stay a couple of days in Punta while we sorted out our gear. At the offices of Adventure Network we had our first opportunity to weigh everything we were going to take, and were astonished to find that it came to more than 500 lbs, way above the 430lbs we had envisaged. In the main, this was due to each of the food packs weighing slightly more than we'd anticipated. Having whittled out a few pieces of equipment that we thought we could do without – the crampons and one of our spare skis – there was nothing to turn to for weight savings but the food itself.

As anyone on a diet will know, fat contains more than twice as many calories as the same weight of protein or carbohydrate. Our day's ration was to consist of a hot cereal start, midday soups and a freeze dried evening meal, all fortified with butter and chocolate bars to make the contents almost 57% fat. This would be much lighter than if we had taken the more normal 35–40% fat diet that most people eat, or the 30% that is considered a healthy target. Previously, we had used a daily intake of about 5,000 calories, twice the normal, but I had not forgotten our weakness at the end of the last North Pole trip, and so, with this expedition likely to be longer still, I reckoned we should eat more. In consultation with Brian Welsby of 'Be-Well', who supplied the food, I decided to increase our intake to 5,500 calories per day through the addition of two more small chocolate bars. This would still be inadequate, for there could be no doubt that we would burn more energy than that, but if we took more food, the sledges would be heavier, harder to pull, and the journey would take longer.

Of course nobody could judge exactly where the optimum compromise lay. As I was convinced that we couldn't pull a weight of 500lbs we had to take a risk and remove one chocolate bar each per day. That meant only 5,200 calories and the hope that this would be enough to limit our overall weight losses to less than twenty pounds each, a figure I thought was sustainable. Any more and we would soon start to weaken.

Even so, it still seemed likely that we would be unable to pull the sledges, and I mentioned this to Annie Kershaw, the Director of Adventure Network, in her office in Punta. I asked her about the possibility of a pick-up or resupply at the Pole if the worst came to the worst, and we discussed the problem in the broadest terms. Later, when I mentioned this conversation to Ran, he was furious. To his way of thinking, any discussion of such matters was 'the leader's job'. Apparently I, fifty per cent of the expedition, had no right to conceive of or to mention alternative plans, even at an informal level. I did not argue with him and apologised. He had always seemed to covet the title of Leader, even though I considered it a joke in the context of a two-man expedition. I could think of us as nothing but entirely equal, but it did not seem worth provoking a quarrel over the matter. The question of leadership was to appear again later in the expedition.

While we were in Punta, we also took the opportunity to make modifications to some of the equipment and clothing. Though all the pieces were designed with the outdoor market in mind, many items were not made for extreme environments and couldn't be handled while wearing several pairs of gloves. Designers hadn't always taken minimum weight into account and there were unnecessary bits of decoration. We spent many days adding additional insulation where necessary, stitching windproofing on vulnerable areas, and tying big toggles on zips and other fasteners.

As in the past, Ran set about these jobs with exuberance. Often highly imaginative in his designer amendments, he would frequently allow his enthusiasm to outpace logic, and modifications would be made that were later regretted. He had the brilliant idea of converting one pair of sunglasses into goggles by removing the side arms that went over the ears and replacing them with an elasticated headband. Sure enough, this proved a useful idea, but in his anxiety to find quickly an elasticated headband, he decided that the best source was the ski-goggles lying beside him. When the job was completed, he proudly showed me the amended item, but his spirits were dashed when I pointed out that he would still need the ski-goggles in windy conditions. He spent the rest of the day hunting around Punta Arenas for suitable material with which to repair the goggles.

Another striking modification, his addition of a large bright blue nose cover to another pair of sunglasses, looked spec-tacularly dotty. Of course, this doesn't matter one bit in the Antarctic, where we certainly weren't planning to be fashion conscious, but Ran insisted on wearing the glasses around the streets of Punta. He cut the most extraordinary figure, walking down the street with this enormous blue beak poking out below white-rimmed glasses, and the local children could hardly fail to point, jeer and laugh. At times, they even followed him round the square like the Pied Piper of Hamelin.

Although I was greatly embarrassed, Ran appeared to be immune to such situations. Embarrassment seems to have been excluded from his make-up. In the past, I had either heard of or witnessed several episodes that would have made the average person squirm, yet Ran never noticed anything unusual. Most recent of these was a story told to me by Ran himself. Just before we had left Britain, he had been making a cafetière of coffee which he planned to drink while in the bath. Unfortunately, when he pushed down the plunger, the cafetière burst, and as he was standing naked in the kitchen at the time, near boiling coffee burnt parts that never should be reached. Remembering his first aid, Ran rushed upstairs, immediately changed the bath water to cold, and sat down in it to obtain instant relief. After fifteen minutes, he tried to get out and found that the relief was only temporary. With the burns still very uncomfortable, he resumed his seated position in the cold water and wondered what to do next. A while later, he decided that he had to see his doctor who had a surgery in central London. Remaining in the bath, he called a taxi on his cellphone and when he heard the doorbell ring, he wrapped a towel around his waist, rushed downstairs and – to the amazement of the taxi driver – asked to be taken directly to Knightsbridge. The taxi driver complied but hit heavy traffic just a few hundred yards from their destination. Ran was in too much discomfort to wait, and left the taxi to run the remainder of the distance, a strange sight as he hurried past Harrods in his white terry loin cloth.

After five days in Punta (three more than originally planned) we went out to the airport to board the old DC6 that ANI used to fly passengers into Antarctica. Boarding with us were two other expeditions: one a group of four Japanese men who were to make a scientific journey to the South Pole; the other a group of four American women who hoped to make an Antarctic crossing as we did although, like Messner, they would not be including the first ice-shelf, and would be re-supplied from the air en route. There were also some professional wildlife photographers and biologists who were to visit the Emperor penguin colonies.

Although large, the aircraft was very cramped inside. Besides expedition cargoes and resupplies for the ANI operation base camp, additional fuel tanks were built into the fuselage to ensure an eighteen-hour flying range, enough to make a round trip to the Antarctic and back to Punta without refuelling. Eagerly we awaited take-off, but as the time ticked by we began to wonder what had gone wrong. After forty-five minutes an engineer told us that there was a leaking fuel valve and that, with no replacement to be found in Punta Arenas, it would take a couple of days to get one from Miami.

The prediction turned out to be hopelessly optimistic. Idling away the time in Punta we saw a week slip past, acutely aware that every day made our chances of success less likely. We devoted our time to eating as much as possible in as many different restaurants as we could find, and as a result began to gain weight rapidly. The extra body weight, a stone each by the time we left Punta Arenas, would later be of great benefit.

At the end of the week the aircraft was functioning, but the weather in Antarctica was bad. Ehrling Kagge arrived from Norway and, continuing in a gentlemanly vein, we met, talked and ate out together on several occasions. I was encouraged when he told me that he personally did not see our ventures as comparable and that he would never view them as a race. Nevertheless he pushed Annie Kershaw to allow him to join our flight, rather than wait for the second on which he was scheduled. For someone who didn't view it as a race, he was very keen to get away at the same time as we did. Annie was unable to help him because our flight was full. When eventually we left, ten days later than scheduled, Ehrling could only wave us off, pressing bars of Norwegian chocolate into our hands to help us on our way. As we departed, I thought that although he was a little too arrogant for my liking, he was a good man and someone I felt I could trust.

The flight to Antarctica took nine hours, the old plane rumbling southward, barely able to fly over some of the high peaks that laid between Punta Arenas and our landing site at Patriot Hills. As we flew we read, ate and slept, and I wrote a letter to Thea.

. . . we are flying South, passing the Peninsula mountains to the left and pack-ice below. The pack in particular reminds me of last time, the cold, the pain and the emptiness. It all frightens me a little bit, not for the fear of my safety, but the knowledge of some of the discomfort to come. It's too late now to back out . . . I haven't been able to see young children, even black-haired as they all are here, without feeling a deep tug inside.

I'm going to have to stop writing for a while. It's getting pretty turbulent and I'm beginning to feel ill. . .

Turbulent? It was wild! Reports were drifting back to us from the cockpit that the weather was worse and deteriorating at Patriot Hills, with winds gusting to 40 knots. Surely we'd have trouble landing on a blue-ice runway in such conditions. I began to think we would find ourselves back in Punta – drinking, eating and getting bored.

My fears were unfounded. Our pilot pressed on, despite the worsening weather, and began his descent parallel to the magnificent Ellesworth mountains. Below and ahead lay a huge area of empty flat blue-ice which had first been found by Giles Kershaw, Annie's husband and one of the pilots on Ran's Transglobe expedition. He had recognised that the smooth ice fields might be used to land wheeled aircraft in Antarctica and this made possible a commercial charter operation. Adventure Network was born and beginning to bear fruit when Giles was killed in a flying accident. The company continued to be operated by his widow and friends.

Landing an aircraft on bare blue-ice is not without its difficulties. High winds roared off the adjacent mountains to blast the ice runway clear of snow, and it was these catabatic winds that now threatened our approach. One minute the air would be almost still, the next gusts reaching gale force hammered at our lurching descent. Suddenly the DC6 was like a roller-coaster. As we dropped lower even wilder gusts picked up the aircraft and threw it sideways. There was a brief touch-down, followed by an enormous leap back into the air. The plane then crabbed and slewed sideways in another flurry before finally making a heavy landing. It felt as if the old airframe would buckle and break with the impact, but the plane gradually slowed and came to a standstill. The passengers gave an audible sigh of relief.

We had stopped in the middle of a clear-blown sea of glass. In howling winds, we unloaded the aircraft as quickly as we could, then made our way over the ice to the Adventure Network base camp. Patriot Hills consisted of a small collection of accommodation tents clustered round a central larger tent that served as kitchen, dining room and lounge. Snow walls defended the little settlement against the fury of the wind.

Tired after our long flight, we were ushered in and, to our surprise, found Giles's 72-year-old mother working in the camp. She welcomed Ran and me as long lost friends and gave us each a bowl of soup and some freshly baked bread. We had not long to linger. Despite it being three o'clock in the morning Chilean time, the weather was fine and in the Antarctic opportunities to fly must never be missed. A ski-equipped Twin Otter was waiting to fly us out to the edge of the Filchner ice-shelf and our starting point.

We hurried through the soup and then spent half an hour filling fuel bottles with petrol for our camp stove. Outside the wind had now reached a screaming 70 knots. The DC6 had already headed back to Punta, for the impending storm could destroy a large aircraft on the ground, whereas the two Twin Otters that were based in Antarctica for the entire season were more resilient and could be lashed down. The pilot for the next stage was keen to get away before the wind became any stronger, and he urged us to pack quickly for take-off. By 4 a.m. we were ready to go and climbed aboard to calls of good luck from the other expeditions and the staff of the camp.

For three hours we flew north-east, dozing fitfully in the cramped seats. The pilot told us that we were approaching Berkner Island and would be flying over the part of the ice-shelf that Ran and I had to cross. Looking down through the window of the Twin Otter, which had been blasted to haze by wind-driven ice crystals, Ran and I did not like what we saw. Before leaving Britain, Ran had consulted the renowned Antarctic geographer, Charles Swithinbank, about our best route. He had recommended this part of the Filchner ice-shelf, but far from being the crevasse-free zone that we had hoped for, the ground appeared dangerously riven with clefts and chasms. The crossing was going to need considerable care. As we completed the last hour of the flight to our start point, I wrote to Thea for the last time.

> . . . *We had to pull our sledges about a mile from the ice runway to the Twin Otter and we did this with only a light load in the sledge. Even with that and the short distance my heart sank as I started to pull. A hundred days of it is going to be dreadfully difficult. I am afraid that, beyond the messages passed via the radio, this will be the last you will hear from me for a while, although if there's any chance, I will get someone to take a letter out from the Pole. That's if we get there of course! I don't rate our chances. Whatever happens, I will be home as soon as possible and although it is unlikely, it would be nice if we were to meet on the Australian side of the world. Thanks again for putting up with me. Keep reminding Callan and Tarn of their eccentric daddy and keep thinking of me. As I walk I will imagine what you are doing at that moment and if you sometimes do the same, we will know that sometimes we are both thinking of each other simultaneously. Above all I promise that I will be careful.*
>
> *All my love, always*
> *Mike.*

Eventually we reached the end of the ice-shelf and, after four or five trial touch-downs, each heavier than the last, the pilot was satisfied with the snow surface and put the plane down in a short area of flat ice adjacent to the frozen sea.

We had arrived at our starting point, two-and-a-half years after first discussing the expedition. Eighteen hundred miles lay before us. I felt like refusing to leave the aircraft.

FOUR

★

Into Another World

WE STEPPED OFF the plane into warm and still conditions, completely different from those we had left at Patriot Hills. The sun was shining and I could feel its warmth through my duvet jacket. The radiance lifted my spirits, but as we unloaded bag after bag of rations, bottle after bottle of fuel, they sank again. Could we even start? The two piles of supplies seemed far too large to be accommodated by our two sledges.

'What do you reckon?' I asked Ran softly, not wanting the pilots to hear me. 'Do you think we can pull them?'

'I don't know,' he replied. 'I'm not even sure we can get it all in. Strap stuff on the top if necessary and let's get started. Once the plane's away we can decide what to do. Try to look confident for the pictures.'

Looking confident was easier said than done. Even with the reduced food we had 485lbs each. No one had ever attempted to pull such loads. It would be so embarrassing if, once in our harnesses, our efforts came to nought and the sledges refused to budge.

Morag, who had accompanied us on the flight to see us off before her long sojourn at Patriot Hills, smiled ruefully. She had heard our whispered conversation and said wryly: 'I'll let the children know I'll be back soon.' She did. That evening when she spoke by radio to Flo at home she gave us just two or three weeks. In her opinion nobody would be able to keep pulling those weights.

Suddenly, a flash of white caught my eye, and a lone snow petrel arrived. These birds, like delicate white doves, are normally seen only around open water. They are viewed

48

as good omens. Although not superstitious, I was heartened by the sight of it, and then thrilled as, hauling on the traces, the sledges slewed round and began to move. The good luck had begun.

I hugged Mo and gave her the letter to Thea. It brought home to me once more what I was doing to my family. Choking back the emotion, I asked Mo to speak to her and give her my love as soon as she could. Then I turned away, embarrassed by the tears that ran down my cheek. I bent low and heaved. The sledge creaked forward and I followed Ran away from the aircraft and down towards the ice-shelf.

It was as well that we were going downhill. The Twin Otter had stopped on the shore of Berkner Island, slightly above the shelf itself, which floated on the sea, so we started with a slope to help us. It allowed us to keep moving for the ten minutes that it took the little plane to become airborne once more. It must have appeared, as we made steady progress towards the south, that we were immensely fit and strong.

The reality was different. It was hard enough pulling the sledges down the slight incline but, when we reached the end of the slope and moved on to the flat ice-shelf, difficult became an understatement. Even straining to the maximum, neither of us could do more than creep forward very slowly, and despite all our training before departure, we couldn't sustain it. Every few hundred yards we would have to stop and rest, allowing our burning thigh muscles to clear the toxic substances that accumulate when over-worked. After four hours of struggling – sweating in a temperature of minus 20°C – we had managed to move only a couple of miles. By that time exhaustion had forced us to stop and make camp. According to Chilean time, it was around midday and we had been up and going for more than thirty hours, while on Greenwich Mean Time, on which we were to operate, it was four o'clock in the afternoon. A short first day seemed reasonable on both counts, and we had taken an extra ration to cover this. With another hundred days to go we felt no guilt.

We rested for a moment, sitting on our sledges, lapping up the low sunshine and basking in our solitude. It was so peaceful, and it felt good to be on our way. To the east and the south, the ice-shelf stretched to the horizon, a flat white plain, punctuated by an occasional gleam of blue, the markings of crevasses. Close by, to our west, was Berkner Island, a line of snow-covered hills. They could have been the fells of an English winter, rising in smooth curves, grey at shadowed bases, glowing on sunlit summits. But they were empty, utterly devoid of animals, plants – or life of any kind.

We made camp as we had done in the north, and although it had been more than two and a half years since our last expedition, it felt routine. The two sledges were drawn up to form a 'V', prow pointing south, the most likely wind direction. Between them we set our tent, anchored by snow-stakes and door to the lee. Everything seemed so familiar, with all the little arrangements that needed to be made inside. Living in a confined, ice-cold tent is an art, and soon we were half-sitting, half-lying on our sleeping bags, feet to the entrance and tea on the brew. The stove was between us, on top of the wooden box in which it travelled, and the box was just big enough to be our table as well as our kitchen. On it our cups stood waiting, along with two large flapjacks. All was eager anticipation, for this was the best part of the day. We were happy and quite comfortable. It felt almost homely.

'How are things at Greenlands?' I asked while waiting for the water to boil.

'Fine,' Ran said. 'We've got all the trees planted and Ginny's cows are doing well. I'm afraid my neighbour did build his ugly barn after all, despite my objections. The Department of the Environment just wouldn't help.'

'What about the ponds?'

'Well, we lined them properly in the end and now we've got ducks, frogs, toads and a great many wildflowers. I've actually been trying to buy the land lower down the stream, to let it run wild as a sort of nature reserve but the farmer won't sell. The only trouble with Greenlands is that Exmoor is so far from London and most other places where I lecture. That's why I need a decent car.'

'You're thinking of something Japanese, are you?' I said, knowing perfectly well that he was a fervent exponent of buying British.

'No, I mean the Rover,' he said. 'I just can't afford to have it taken off the road again.'

'You're not still collecting speeding tickets?' Ran was always being fined or banned from driving.

'I haven't had one since the last time in London,' he said. 'I thought that was a stiff enough fine considering.'

'What do you mean?' I asked.

'Well, I was driving along the Embankment by the Thames, and only doing about fifty or sixty. It wasn't obvious that it was a thirty mile an hour limit. I was on my way to the theatre to see "The Woman in Black" – marvellous play, you should see it...'

'But what would you expect along the river in central London? It would *have* to be a thirty mile limit.'

'Yes, that's what the policeman said. But it was only built up on one side.'

The next couple of days were fine and warm, and to ease ourselves into the expedition, we pulled for seven hours, then eight hours, aiming to increase to ten or twelve later. At first the hauling was tough, as back-breaking as when we first set off, and we had to make constant stops for rest. But surprisingly, within these two days, I began to find it easier and was able to pull with much less frequent pauses. I wondered why, since the sledges were negligibly lighter and the training from the manhauling wouldn't have been of benefit so quickly. The fact is that when muscles are first asked to do a new kind of work, they are unused to it and so cannot coordinate the strength of all their fibres. Then, quite rapidly, they learn to do so, and I guessed that this was the source of our amazing gain in strength.

There was only one dampener: when we came to our second soup stop on the very first full day, we were dismayed to find our first equipment failure.

'Ran, is your soup warm?' I asked.

'No. Absolutely stone cold, and pretty disgusting.'

So was mine. To obtain a high calorie intake at low weight, even the soup had added fat – all very well when hot, but not so nice when congealed into cold globs.

51

'It must be the thermos,' I said, 'but they're meant to be unbreakable.'

Ran laughed. 'Not with you about. No thermos is safe from your talents.'

I smiled. He was referring back to the very first journey we had made, when I had managed to break both thermos flasks. At that time they had been made of glass. The first had broken because I didn't appreciate how rough the terrain was going to be and had put the flask in my sledge, lodged fairly loosely on top of my load. It had smashed on the first day. I was terribly embarrassed and expected Ran to blow up. On unsupported expeditions, you cannot afford to break things. In fact he had been remarkably good about it – more evidence of Ran's easy going nature. Then I broke the other. Not the next day, but still within a week of starting. I was behind, and since Ran was walking back to me at the breaks, he had given me the second thermos to carry. Now I stowed it much more carefully, wrapped up in my sleeping bag, but again one morning we found our drink full of fragmented glass. I was horrified. One flask was careless but two was unforgivable.

If I were Ran I would have been very angry, but with admirable self-control, he merely asked for suggestions as to what other container we could use. One possibility had been an empty fuel bottle, but they were of metal and so the contents would get cold so quickly that they might well have frozen. There had been only one alternative. When camping in the extreme cold, it was common practice among climbers and travellers alike to have a 'pee' bottle – a container you could use conveniently even inside your sleeping bag. Ours was made of plastic, and so a fairly good insulator. With luck, wrapped up in a sleeping bag, it would keep our drink reasonably warm. When I suggested it to Ran, he was dubious and thought the contamination would make us ill. I assured him that urine was quite sterile and that we would come to no harm. Reluctantly Ran agreed that there was nothing else we could do.

It is interesting in retrospect that neither of us considered giving up using it as a pee bottle. We had just accepted that, in the circumstances, we would do something that normally would seem abhorrent. The system certainly worked. On that trip we were using a carbohydrate-rich drink called 'Pre-Stress', designed to give athletes a burst of energy before competition, and it not only stayed liquid but kept pretty warm for a couple of hours. With a good shake of the bottle before filling, there wasn't even a taint to the taste. Inevitably it became known as 'Pee-Stress'.

On our subsequent expeditions we took unbreakable metal flasks. Until now we had never had further trouble.

'No, it wasn't me,' I said. 'This one must have been a dud before we started. Next time we'll test them first.'

'Oh good,' said Ran. 'I can hardly wait for next time.'

At the end of the second day we entered the crevasse field that we had seen from the air. When we made camp, we pitched the tent only twenty yards from a huge open crack, but overnight the wind rose and by morning there was snow blowing from the north and a whiteout completely obscured the rift. Discretion being the better part of valour, we made the tent more secure and retired back inside. Then we dozed for a further four hours with frequent checks on the weather. We were anxious to start as soon as we could. Not only were we wasting hauling time, but the wind offered the potential to try our up-ski sails.

Ran now viewed these sails in a different light. On the flight out he had read Messner's book and so came to agree with my conclusion – an unsupported journey across Antarctica was probably impossible without wind assistance. Even with the wind it was improbable. He had therefore given up any resistance to their use, and became as keen as I was to learn whether they were effective. Winds from the north would be unusual once we left the coastal area, and so this might be our last chance to test them for many many weeks. If we knew how well they worked, it would be much easier to make plans for the far end of the journey, when we hoped they would be of most benefit.

At around two in the afternoon, the storm began to die down and the crevasse reappeared. We were outside and started packing at once. Then we unfurled our sails and, with the confidence of the truly unskilled, put on our skis and tied into both sledge and the sail harnesses. After a few poor starts we were up, the parachutes inflated ahead and pulling hard at our waists. Their effectiveness was immediately apparent. They worked wonderfully in terms of pulling us and the sledges, but it was difficult to control either speed or direction. The idea is that you can edge your skis and sail up to 45 degrees on either side of the wind and, by controlling the size of a central hole in the chute, regulate speed. It is not so easy in practice. With a heavy sledge dragging behind, you are limited to about 25 degrees off the wind, and even this can put an enormous strain on the legs and back. We found that initiating a change in direction was a slow business and speed control negligible.

To inflate the sail, I had to pull on a control cord which closed the centre hole while the canopy was still on the ground. Then, a flick at one of the risers allowed the edge to catch the wind and, almost immediately, the thing rose up like a huge coloured beast and I was off, racing across the ice, and desperately opening the centre hole to try and slow down. It had no apparent effect. Full speed was maintained right up to the stage when the hole was so big that the sail wouldn't fly at all, at which point it would collapse and promptly tangle itself up. This necessitated a period of frustrating and intensely cold macrame, inevitably with bare fingers. Furthermore, while I was hurtling forwards, the sail flew very close to the ground, almost completely obscuring the view ahead and catching on small surface features to tangle itself up anyway. Although they were clearly of great potential benefit, the sails were going to need considerable skill in their use, and they would be limited by strong winds or difficult terrain.

All the same, they were compulsive. Compared with the toil of manhauling, to be pulled forward at high speed was a delight so intense that to ignore it, merely because it was difficult and dangerous, was near impossible. Instead of stopping once we had learned of the difficulties, we went on, in strong winds and poor visibility, regardless of being in a crevassed zone. It was a stupid thing to do, but we were desperate to take advantage of a ride that we knew might not occur again for a couple of months. The light was poor and it was impossible to discern the tell-tale dips in the snowfields that marked hidden crevasses. It was also difficult to be sure that rising ground

6 Mount Erebus, Antarctica, on the 'Footsteps' expedition 1985/86

7 Morag, our radio
  operator, at the
  Emperor penguin
  colony

8 Unloading the Twin
  Otter, November 1992

9 Mike and Ran setting
  off for an 1,800-mile
  unsupported walk

wasn't obscuring the view. It was the latter that almost spelt disaster.

Ran was just ahead of me when I saw him fall just to the left of a long open crack – a blue slash in the white that joined ground to sky. Ahead of him, it looked firm and so, steering left, I carried on, aiming to pass close by. I didn't realise that he had not fallen by chance. He had thrown himself over when he had seen that the crack extended in front of him and his chute had collapsed, a coloured flag, draped over the entrance to an icy coffin. I was going much faster when I saw it, and the gaping chasm filled my vision with its darkness and my mind with horror. I tore at the control cord release, but it was far too late, and as my gloved hands fumbled fruitlessly at the toggle, I heard Ran shout, 'No-o-o . . .!' – the short word extending into a long wail that followed me over the edge as my mind echoed the same pointless denial and I rushed towards black depths that lay to either side.

I didn't fall freely. Instead I hung beneath the partially inflated chute and swung forward to smash into the wall on the far side of the cleft. It was rough blue-ice and my forehead struck hard, dazing me slightly. I scrabbled at the wall, trying to grasp at something to hold, anything rather than be pulled down. It was useless. Although I did get my hand around a protrusion, it was smooth as glass, and the weight of the sledge came on to me, ripped me off and I fell backwards. At that moment, I was sure I was going to meet my death. I knew that behind there was nothing; I had seen the bottomless pit.

I was wrong. Instead of plummeting into the darkness, I dropped another ten feet or so before I landed hard on a surface, my back crashing painfully into the front of my sledge. For a moment I lay still, winded, confused, scarcely able to believe my luck. Then I looked around, not daring to move, trying to assess my situation. I was perched on a narrow snow platform, where the crevasse had been choked by drift. It was about twenty feet down, and the walls of shimmering blue rose almost vertically above me. To either side, just a few feet away, the crevasse was open and the same walls went on down, darker and darker until they passed out of sight. The blackness beckoned. In front of me, just beyond my feet, the snow surface was punctured by a yard-wide hole, another entrance to the void. I could see from its edges that my platform was horribly thin. It was a precarious position and I gazed up at the band of sky, wondering how to get out.

'Mike!' The shout came from above. 'Are you okay?'

I had forgotten about Ran. He had seen me disappear, and perhaps half a minute had passed. Later he told me that he was sure I was dead.

'I'm fine,' I shouted back in reassurance. 'Fine, but it's not too clever and I need some help.'

Although I was virtually unhurt, the alloy traces of my sledge, rigid tubes that made the sledge turn and follow me closely, were crumpled and smashed beyond repair. The sledge itself was also damaged, the carbon-fibre/kevlar shell cracked at the front and creased across the middle. Still, the hull was essentially in one piece and we could go on if only I could get it and myself out safely. I tried to move, but my skis were wedged beneath me, dug awkwardly into the fragile snow, and when I struggled I heard pieces of my bridge falling away beneath. I broke into a sweat that instantly turned to frost on my forehead. If I tried too hard I would destroy this thin meringue that supported me. I didn't know what to do. I couldn't move with the skis on, but in boots alone it would be very easy to fall through. It seemed hopeless but I had no choice – I had to take them off, keep close to the wall and hope for the best.

I unstrapped one of the skis and pulled the foot free. I was half-kneeling, with the knee of the ski-shod foot on the snow and the ski tip stuck in behind me. I tentatively put some weight on the booted foot. The surface was quite soft and it sunk in, but then held. Slowly I pressed more heavily, intending to stand up and then pull the ski out from behind me. Without warning, the foot suddenly went through and I pitched forwards. My mind made another silent cry of denial – no, not *now*! It was heard. My face hit the snow and a hole appeared, my outstretched arm went through it, but the bridge still held as dislodged pieces of ice fell away and disappeared under my gaze. I felt sick with fear, transfixed, and had to quash the panic that flooded up within me.

'You've got the rope, Mike. Tie yourself on and get it up to me.'

Of course ... I had to get the rope. I eased back into a kneeling position and released the other binding while staying with my weight on the ski. Then I turned round and slowly bent over towards the sledge. I couldn't reach the sledge zip without moving and had to lean quite hard on the hull as I did so. As my weight came on to it, the sledge lurched downwards, and life stopped. Underneath me I heard the sound of more ice falling.

'Christ! This is no place to stick around...' I muttered, and then I almost laughed at the inadequacy of my verbal assessment.

I undid the sledge cover and the rope was right in front of me. I had put it there in case I needed to get Ran out. He had been ahead, and we followed a policy of the rear man always carrying the rope.

'Ran, I'll try to throw it up,' I shouted, my voice sounding alien with tension. 'Can you get over the crack to the other side.'

'Yes, I won't be a minute,' the answer came from an invisible source. 'I reckon I can cross about fifty yards away.'

I kept quite still as I heard footsteps receding. Looking along the length of the crevasse, I could see that thirty or forty yards away the blue ravine became a black tunnel, roofed over by another snow bridge on the surface. That was where Ran was going to cross. Underneath, there was an immense emptiness. My God! Was that really what we'd been crossing?

Ran reappeared at the other lip. 'Okay,' he said. 'Chuck it up here.'

I took the rope and tied one end to one of the carrying loops of the sledge cover, and I also tied myself on about halfway along. Then I checked that the other coils were free and threw it with all my strength. It snaked up and over the top and I saw Ran catch it. As the rope brushed the lip some pieces fell and went straight through my support. It really was very thin in places, and another sickening wave of panic gripped my stomach. I had to force it down, and then shouted far too loudly.

'Anchor it off on your sledge or something and I'll throw up some of the food and stuff. We'll never get it out of here without reducing the weight.'

I heard Ran's muffled acknowledgement. He was already doing it and didn't need to be told. When he was ready, I began to unload, trying not to move my feet, or to press too heavily on the sledge. I threw up one ration, one fuel bottle, one piece of equipment at a time. Each one disappeared as Ran caught them at the edge twenty feet above and piled them safely to one side. As I worked, concentrating on the activity, the inner churning subsided, but all the time I was conscious of just how little lay between me and the gulf.

It took about twenty minutes to empty the load and then Ran called down. 'Just hang on a moment and I'll get in a position to pull.' He tied himself up close to his sledge anchor and then braced his feet against the snow while taking up the slack to give me a tight rope. Then, with him pulling, and me climbing as best I could, I slowly scaled the wall of the crevasse at a point where it wasn't quite so steep. Finally, grunting with the effort, I emerged from the gateway to death and lay panting on the surface, my cheek on the cool snow. I felt a strange combination of elation and joy mixed with a crushing sense of vulnerability. My life had been so close to an end and I thought of my children, fatherless into the future.

Neither of us spoke for a moment. There was nothing to say. We pulled up the empty sledge in silence, watching as the snow bridge on which I had lain collapsed, rumbling into eternity. I turned and looked ahead. The sun was shining now and the wind had dropped. The scene was remarkably peaceful. Then Ran looked at me and saw that I was shocked by what had happened. Just for a moment he put his arm around my shoulders in the briefest of reassuring gestures. It was the most that our upbringing and a stiff upper lip would allow. He smiled.

'I don't know what I'd have told Thea,' he said. 'Shall we go?'

There was no wind for further sailing and so we resumed manhauling. I was now pulling on rope instead of the rigid traces which had been buckled and consigned to the black depths of the crevasse from which I'd escaped. When we started to go downhill after the Pole in two months' time, ropes would allow the sledge to catch up with me and knock me off my feet. Still, that was a long way ahead and we might never get as far. For the moment we had more acute worries. Looking back at the sledge, I noticed that it flexed as I moved and realised that we would be lucky if it held together. If it fell apart now, or even soon, there was no way in which we would be able to carry its load. One or even one and a half sledges wouldn't have the capacity to sustain us both all the way. I could only hope that it would last. In any case, it was a gorgeous evening in the sunshine and if a break did precipitate a premature end to the expedition, I didn't mind. I was just happy to be alive.

That night in the tent we encountered another problem while I was trying to change the fuel bottle and couldn't get the new one to fit.

'Ran, I can't get the stove pump to screw into the bottle. It keeps going cross-threaded. Have you got the spare pump?'

'It's in the blue stuff bag,' he replied, 'but have you tried a different bottle?'

'Well, I've tried to put the empty one back, and I can't get that to fit now. It was okay before. Now it's as if the two threads are different.'

When I had first assembled the stove there had been no difficulty; now neither the pump nor the spare pump would fit into any bottle. Ran had a go but was unable to do any better.

'We're in real trouble,' I said. 'If we can't use the stove we're stuffed.'

Without a suitable cooker we were in immediate danger. There was no other way of using our fuel effectively. Even if we called for an urgent pick-up, flying in Antarctica is never a certainty and we might have to wait for a week or more. If we were unable to melt snow for drinking or cooking, that might prove too long.

'Surely you can cobble something together,' said Ran.

Cobbling was one of Ran's strengths. His years of expeditions had taught him that usually something could be done, even without specialised equipment.

'We could try it cross-threaded with two washers, using the one off the spare. But I doubt if we can make it seal.

It certainly won't be the safest stove around.'

My words were prophetic. Although I managed to make it work by accepting the cross-threading and putting in an extra 'O' ring, the stove had not long been pumped up when suddenly I smelt petrol.

'Christ, Ran, the stove!'

It was too late. With a loud *WHOOMPH* it went up and the whole tent was engulfed in flames. Ran moved like lightning. Whether through quick thinking or self-preservation, I'm not sure, but before I knew it, he had ripped open the door zips and was out. I flung the burning stove, the cook-pot and the base box after him and Ran, in underwear and bare feet, buried them in snow to put out the flames.

Fortune had smiled again. A fire is the Antarctic dweller's greatest fear, whether living in a tent or a permanent base. With it, all in one go you can lose your accommodation, warmth, clothing and communications. With both the radio and satellite beacon in the tent, a moment more could have reduced us to semi-clothed, possibly injured individuals with no means of letting our position be known. We had to be more careful. Making the stove/fuel bottle union entirely safe was impossible and we were going to be vulnerable for as long as the journey continued. From that time on, we pumped the stove with excessive care.

After returning from the expedition I was to learn that the stove manufacturer had made a small change to the thread of the pumps in order to prevent people from using the fuel bottles we had taken instead of the manufacturer's own. Having used the other connection for years, I hadn't thought to check it. I still don't know how I managed to put the two together on the very first bottle.

The next few days took us through more heavily cre-vassed areas. We avoided the obvious holes and travelled roped together. Nervously we crossed snow bridges spanning the dark depths, and although the rope was reassuring, we lived in dread that one of us would go through with his full load. We were never confident that the other would be able to bear the weight. Each day we hoped to reach better ground, but as the first week passed the going remained unchanged. Travelling roped slowed us down and only reduced the risks. Eventually a decision was made to turn from the direct line and go in close to the shore of Berkner Island where less disrupted ice might offer the prospect of moving more freely.

There was an immediate improvement closer in where we found no crevasses and felt secure enough to dispense with the rope. We began to adopt a regular daily routine. I would start off leading, and then we would change each hour until we had completed an eight-hour day. However, the length of the hours was not constant, and each day we added five minutes or so to some of the periods. By doing that the early hours of the day became longer and longer and our work time extended to ten or eleven hours.

The pulling was utterly draining. Small promontories from Berkner Island forced us to haul up and down undulations, and on the ascents it was often impossible to keep going. Our thigh muscles burnt out with the strain and again we had to make stops to let them recover. Nevertheless we were reasonably happy and began to settle into this strange way of life and to make the mental adaptations that would permit us to carry on with it for the next three months. The most important adjustment was to day-dreaming. Only then was it possible to detach oneself from the drudgery. Once the crevassed area was passed, I found myself drifting into worlds of my own making for most of the day, only returning to the world of toil to check the compass occasionally or to swap leads with Ran. Many of these day-dreams I would start quite deliberately, picking on a topic and then thinking it through step by step.

Most commonly, I thought of my family and never without eyes filling. I would do so much for them when I got home. My wife would have lots of her own free time to make up for my absence. It must be so hard for her, looking after the kids on her own, with little adult company day in day out. Knowing her, I was sure she would rather have swapped places. She had seen the Antarctic when she came down as a crew member on the ship to collect us from the Footsteps expedition. Then, of course, the ship had been crushed by the ice and her voyage was curtailed. Still, it meant that she could picture my circumstances, and that probably helped her. Most men couldn't have coped with her domestic situation. I had taken on the kids for three weeks the previous summer when Thea had gone travelling in Mexico and Belize. They had nearly driven me crazy, even with the help of my mother who stayed with us for much of the time. I had learned that looking after children was no easy option, and they had learned that Daddy could lose his rag. Now of course, when I returned, my children would never find me frustrated or annoyed and I would play with them constantly. On Saturdays we would all go out for treats, visiting zoos, cinema matinées and McDonald's. We would have so much fun together, and of course there would be the holidays. I planned – enough to last a lifetime.

I also thought about the house and all the jobs I would do when I got back. Somehow I felt that I would be super-efficient and that everything I had left for so long would be completed. In my mind I travelled round the house putting up shelves in every room, painting and decorating in a way that I could never hope to match in reality. The interior, the exterior, every aspect of the house would become spick and span in a fervour of do-it-yourself. The garden was going to be spectacular. I would return at the end of winter and there would be so many jobs to do. No matter, they would all be done in no time. In my mind I planned the vegetable garden and planted all the seeds; I cleared out the greenhouse and altered the front garden path. Perhaps most important, I built the Wendy house that I had been promising the children for so long. I sat in it with them, drinking tea, while they drank their Ribena.

My old car was another source of distraction. For many months prior to my departure on the expedition, I had occasionally grabbed a moment to work on this twenty-five-year-old MG. It was now partially restored and lying idle in the garage. Methodically I would think my way through all that it needed, starting, strangely enough, at the back with a new rear bumper, and finishing at the front with the suspension. In between, everything old would be replaced and everything mechanical overhauled. It was to be an overhaul so thorough that in reality it would have taken me years, yet

I was going to do it in the few days before I went back to work.

Thinking of that car reminded me of another. Before leaving home, we had assembled all the expedition kit in the basement car park of an office block in London where Ran used to work. He and I met there for the day and waded through boxes of clothing and gear obtained by our equipment sponsor, Blacks. There had been so much stuff that, after sorting out what we needed and packing it off to KLM, who were to fly it to South America, we found ourselves with a sizeable excess, especially when added to the gear that had been pulled out from previous expeditions. Having promised to leave the store empty, we shared out all the spare stuff and put it into our cars – in my case, a small Vauxhall Astra which I had bought to use temporarily during the MG's renovation. With the MG almost completed and the expedition about to depart, I had arranged to sell the Astra to a colleague the following day. The small car was packed to the roof with all the boxes I had pushed in, and there were skis crossing from the back and resting beneath the windscreen on the passenger side. All this kit obscured my view, and I forgot that I had parked adjacent to a concrete pillar. As I reversed and swung the car round, I heard a sickening crunch as I stoved in the passenger door. Needless to say, I was not best pleased at the time, and even as I hauled across the ice the thought made me cringe.

For most of the days on the ice-shelf the sun shone, the weather was calm, and we had no more northerly winds to carry us on our way. By Polar standards, it was at the same time relatively warm – minus 20°C – but we were wearing little clothing, and when we stopped for soup after three and six hours, the chill got through to us within five minutes and we wanted to move on. We did have one spell of bad weather on Day 11, when a southerly gale kept us in the tent. In view of our critical logistics, we decided not to use a ration that day, and spent most of it dozing and becoming increasingly hungry. At around 7 p.m. we ate a pack of porridge mixed with oxtail soup, food that we had saved from an earlier ration pack.

'Wow, that tastes pretty strange,' said Ran. 'Ginny could have cooked it.'

He was certainly right about the taste – an odd combination of sweet and salt.

'That's a bit unfair,' I said. 'As I recall, Ginny's a good cook. At least, the food's great if you can keep the dogs off it.'

When you visited Ran's home, meals were often eaten under the jealous gaze of five enormous black hounds.

'Don't you criticise my dogs,' Ran said with a laugh. 'They happen to be a highly obedient group of monsters. But you're right. I do actually love Ginny's cooking. How's Thea getting on?' He recalled that when I first met Thea she couldn't even boil an egg. Food simply held no interest for her.

'Well, it's much better than it was,' I said. 'She does quite a lot of cooking now, though she still won't test her skills on visitors, so any dinner parties are firmly in my court.'

We finished our improvised supper in silence. Then Ran made a suggestion.

'How about a game of draughts?' he said. 'We could draw a board on the lid of the stove box and play with the pee samples.'

'Good idea, but I'm not very good at it. You'll have to remind me of the rules.'

We drew out the board and set up the little urine containers that were used for nightly samples. Ran had the full ones, I the empty. After a few games, Ran wanted to know about chess. To my amazement, he had never played chess before and so, after supplementing the urine pawns with rough drawings of Bishops and Knights and the rest on scraps of paper, I spent some time explaining the game. Eventually we played on into the sunlit night with the wind howling and the tent shaking. It must have made a curious scene.

Along with the drain of the work, there was also the discomfort. In the evening we ached in every muscle and joint, and overnight the pains didn't disappear; they were just compounded by stiffness. The harnesses chaffed our waists, even through our clothing, and our feet, not yet hardened to the constant abuse, developed hot spots and blisters. Soon we both had raw areas over the hips and the soles of our feet were great painful erosions. Every time we started walking, our feet would burn, as if on hot coals, but later, as long as one didn't stop, one became inured to it.

With the ozone-hole firmly established over the South Pole, Antarctica is a terrible place for ultra-violet radiation. It rapidly burns sensitive areas, and our lips soon became blistered, cracked and sore. I had my share of this problem, but Ran's was far worse. As well as burning areas directly, ultra-violet light can also re-activate the virus responsible for cold-sores. This lies dormant in susceptible individuals, and Ran had had such sores in the past. Now they returned with a vengeance, and his lips became ravaged and swollen, a mass of open ulcers that wept constantly. In the evening, as we ate directly out of a shared cooking pot, they would bleed into the food – something that I found quite distasteful. Overnight the lips would stick together so that in the morning he had to ease them apart with a finger before he could speak or even smile.

Desperately he tried all our different sun screens, the best available on the market, but his lips were no better. Finally he resorted to cutting off a piece from the end of the leg of his fleece trousers. Then he stiffened the circle of fabric with some wire, and attached some elastic to hold it on to his face. It created a total lip protector which he called a 'dodo beak', and it proved to be highly effective. In combination with the blue nose, this bright purple contraption would have reduced the children of Punta to hysterics.

FIVE

★

A Question of Leadership

BY THE END of two weeks we had travelled about 150 miles. This was not at all bad for the start of an expedition with such heavy weights, but we were acutely aware that for overall success we would have to average some 17 miles per day. There would be a lot to make up. On Day 14 we reached the point at which we had no choice but to turn and head for the mainland. To travel any farther along the coast of the island would be to go too far west. With the earlier crevasse experience still fresh in my mind, I have to admit that the thought of casting out on to the open ice-shelf frightened me.

My fears were well founded. When we left Berkner Island behind our route took us across what appeared to be a featureless flat white plain. Yet, as I led the way, about fifty yards in front of Ran, there was a sudden muffled bang and ahead of me a plume of snow crystals rose into the air as if someone had triggered a small explosion. Then there came a long deep rumbling, felt as much as heard, and ten yards in front, apparently solid ground began to open. Slowly, and then with increasing momentum, a black zig-zag crack split the white surface, widening as the edges fell in upon themselves. Within moments, it had become a ten yard wide deep fissure exactly where I would have walked, and as I watched, it steadily extended for about forty yards in either direction. For several seconds after it had appeared, I could still feel through my feet the rumbling of the huge ice blocks as they tumbled and dropped into the very heart of the shelf. It was like a scene from an earthquake movie, when cracks open to swallow people, cars and buildings, and after my previous experience it shook me

66

to the core and once again I felt sweat frost upon my brow and my heart beating wildly in my tightened chest.

Where else around me did these hidden chasms lie? Which way would take us safely out of here? I could see no clues, but I had my answers quickly. Although everywhere looked smooth, with no sign that the ground was hollow, similar chasms lay all around and no route was safe. As soon as I turned to head parallel to the newly opened rift, there was another muffled rumbling and another crack unzipped. This time it was back beyond Ran, in an area that we had both just crossed. Then there was another, and another, and our smooth plain became a heaving nightmare. We roped up, both now terrified. The ground was alive and blue gaping mouths opened before us, behind us, around us. On one occasion, as we made our way forward one step at a time, probing the snow with hard stabs of the ski-sticks, a canyon appeared between us, and I turned to see my tracks fragmenting and crashing into a void spanned by our pathetically thin rope. These crevasses were so big that they could have taken us both at once, and all were invisible before they opened.

I couldn't understand why they were there. Crevasses normally occur where glacial ice flows over a convexity so that the surface is stressed and breaks. Here, out on the ice-shelf, there seemed to be no good reason for them, although I guessed that there was some submarine cause, perhaps a rise in the sea floor hundreds of feet below us. But without any visible sign of their origin, we could take no obvious course to get away from them and all we could do was doggedly press on, heading south and praying that the disruption was localised. Fortunately, it was. After two hours – beyond doubt the most frightening of our lives – the cracking came to an end and slowly our fears began to settle as we set out across a now quiet flat white plain, following a compass bearing for landfall.

Behind us, the island receded and we became surrounded by a calm and empty sea. No man, no animal, no bird, not even an insect would have passed this way before us and the same would apply to the hundreds of miles that still lay ahead to the Pole. It was a strange thought and quite different from my previous experiences. With the 'Footsteps of Scott', my forays had been close to the coast and the men from Scott's and Shackleton's expeditions and the more modern scientists from the American and New Zealand bases at McMurdo Sound who had preceded us. There had also been animals and birds and even in the depths of winter, crossing the sea-ice under the stars and the aurora, seals could be found lying by the tide cracks, waiting for the return of the sun. At Cape Crozier, which I had visited with Roger Mear and Gareth Wood when we repeated Scott's 'Worst Journey in the World', there were the Emperor penguins. They had stood in the deeply frozen mid-winter night, enduring weeks without food, as they followed the drive of nature to lay and incubate their eggs in bitter darkness. Only then could their chicks hatch early enough in the brief Antarctic summer to grow strong before the next winter came. It was an extraordinary sight, and a privilege to witness such a wonder of the world.

Up north there had also been animals to see while we dragged our sledges over those terrible broken floes, especially seals by areas of open water. With the seals came the threat of Polar bears and we lived in constant fear of these efficient hunters whenever we saw their freshly trodden trails. Wrapped up as we were with balaclavas and hoods, we would never have heard them as they stalked up from behind, and our flares and gun would probably have been useless. But Ran and I never were attacked, and only Flo and Mo had close contact with the wildlife. Located on the coast in our remote base camps, they saw bears, caribou, hares and foxes, and on one occasion even adopted a local wolf. She was a lone pure-white female which started to live around their camp, scavenging what she could. At first they were nervous of her and went out armed whenever she was around, but later they forgot their anxieties and Edna, as they called her, became a friend who would try and eat their boots, even when they wore them. Of course, being unarmed when dangerous animals roam can have its disadvantages. One day when Flo went to the loo in a little shack away from the main huts, Edna was joined by her friends. It was eleven hours before he dared to come out.

Having moved away from the undulations close to Berkner

Island, the sledge became more manageable and I began to be optimistic about the future. If it were as easy as this here, when our loads still weighed so much, surely later on we would steam along and those big distances we needed would be forthcoming. I began to pull faster, but Ran was not so happy. Over the first couple of weeks, I had had some trouble keeping up with him, but now things were reversed. For the first time since we had joined forces on expeditions, it was he who was finding the pulling harder. He felt it sorely. During thirty years of expeditioning, his phenomenal physical strength, supported by his fearsome determination, had never been challenged. Now, although only marginally slower, he had to accept the effects of his age and suffered inner torment as he tried to come to terms with it. It was a difficult experience and he reacted in two opposing fashions. On the one hand he would complain bitterly, even aggressively, that I was going too fast, while on the other he would be over-apologetic about his slowness. We discussed it frequently.

'It's really no problem, Ran. We're going pretty well, in fact faster than the Footsteps team, or Messner at this stage. I quite like having less pressure on me. Anyway, at the end of an hour you're usually just behind me.'

'Yes, I'm just behind,' he replied, 'but at what cost? I can't stop to make clothing adjustments, or to have a pee, because if I do I will miss the train. Once I've missed it, I can't catch up. And anyway, getting behind is terrible for my morale.'

I couldn't see the difficulty. Brief pauses were not a problem if we kept going at a reasonable pace for the rest of the time.

'But I'm happy to wait for you,' I said. 'Just ask whenever you need to do anything and I'll stop. It doesn't bother me. In fact I welcome the breaks. Alternatively I could start to take a bit off your load. It would slow me up, make you faster, and all in all we would get on quicker.'

'No ... I don't want to do that,' he said hesitantly, 'I'd rather you just adopted a pace that I can maintain. You go too quickly for your own good, and certainly for mine. The answer is my Polar plod. That's what will see us to the Pole in good condition.'

Ran's 'Polar plod' was very slow, the steady tramp that he adopted when leading. His rationale was that it avoided burning ourselves out, but after a few days of it, I had begun to find it frustrating.

'Well, I can try,' I said, 'but it's pretty difficult to go at any speed other than the one that feels right. I remember you saying something similar to me when we were up in the Arctic.'

'Yes, in those days when I wasn't such a geriatric,' he said sadly. 'I should never have come on this trip. I should've left it for you to do with someone like Kagge.'

'Ran, you don't need to think like that. As I said, we're going pretty fast and your age is not a big deal. The most likely thing to cock up an expedition like this is trouble with relationships, or someone just not being able to hack it. Although, no doubt, there'll be times when we're nearly spitting on this trip, at least you're someone I can get along with, and who I know will never give up. I rely on your determination. I'd rather have that than be with someone who would go a few hundred yards more every day. If you remember, that's why we decided to stick to the two of us.'

There was a time when we had wondered whether to take some additional members into our two-man team, men who could share the fixed weights of the cooking, communication and safety gear, and hence reduce individual sledge weights. But the most likely reason for failure in an enterprise such as we proposed, was incompatibility, or the mental collapse of an individual. Every additional man would be an unknown that would make these problems more likely. Past experience had taught us that Ran and I got on well and that we could probably keep going for a long time. The additional benefits did not outweigh the risk, and we had decided that once more we would go alone.

'Thanks,' he said, 'but when you're racing out in front, I hate you.'

'Don't worry,' I retorted. 'I more than hated you in the Arctic. I'll tell you about it some time.'

Our journey continued and empty day followed empty day. As a consequence of Ran's speed, all physical pressure was taken off me and I felt wonderful. If I needed to stop

70

and rest my legs while leading, I didn't feel guilty that I held him up, and if I stopped for a pee while following, I could easily catch up again. It was also good for my vanity – not the there-and-then of finding myself faster, but the thought of the future. After we had got back to the U.K. from our last expedition, Ran had seemed to forget that I was as fast as he was for most of the journey and instead, in each telling of the story, he had become more and more convinced that I was always a distant black dot behind him. Indeed even the story of how he had rescued me from the sea when I fell into a crack had changed. It had been as bad as the crevasse accident this time, a terrible episode that didn't need any alteration.

It happened after we had ditched the sledges and I was struggling along with a crushing back pack. I was following on foot where Ran had just passed on skis and so I was much more likely to break through. Suddenly I had gone down. It came as such a shock. There had been no sign of the crack yet it was about five feet across, hidden by snow blown by the wind into a delicate carapace. I dropped straight through the thin ice that lay upon the dark water and went under, swallowing cold brine as I involuntarily gasped. Then I popped up again, floating with the air trapped in my clothing. I spluttered and wiped the water from my face, surprised at finding myself afloat and wondering why it didn't feel cold. That quickly changed. It was only a moment before the icy water poured through my clothing, so cold that it hurt – a tight band round my chest. I realised that I had to get out quickly and I shouted for Ran while looking up at the smooth sides of the crack. They were vertical, and I was about four feet below the top. I could see no place to climb them and I shouted again more urgently.

'Ran ... Raaaan!'

No reply. He had been close by when I fell, stopped about twenty yards away, but he had been facing the other way and the wind was blowing. Maybe he had set off walking without looking back. I began to panic. I couldn't help it.

How could I get out? The cold would be too much. Water could rob the body of all warmth and strength in seconds. It was all going to end. It just wasn't fair. Stop! ... Think clearly for a moment. Take a grip. There must be a way.

Obviously I couldn't climb out with the backpack. It was rapidly becoming sodden and far too heavy. I had to get it off in the water, but every time I tried I sank. My fingers were already numbing with the cold and would soon lose their grip altogether. Then I heard Ran calling.

'Mike, Mike! Are you okay?'

Thank God! He hadn't disappeared after all. He was there.

'Here, grab the stick.' He lay down and lowered a ski pole full length. I seized it, but as he pulled I realised that there was no chance.

'I can't! I've got to get the sack off.' I could hear the fear in my voice.

There was only one way to do it. I had to let go, take a breath and go under, fumbling the straps from my shoulders as I sank. Just as my lungs were bursting, I broke free. The sack was off and I pushed back to the surface.

'Quick! Take the sack or it'll sink.'

Ran hooked his ski-stick into the hoisting strap and up it went. Then it was my turn, and I grasped the stick and pulled again. I only came slightly out of the water. The weight of my sodden clothing was still too great and there was no way that Ran could heave me out. I fell back exhausted. My whole body was beginning to chill and my muscles were losing function.

'Come on, Mike. Come on!'

It was all very well for him to shout, but how could I come on? What could I do with only a few seconds left? To my right the crack narrowed – perhaps there I could get out. Perhaps if I bridged with my legs at the same time.

'Ran, I'll move. Let's try there, where it's narrower.'

We both moved along, and Ran lowered the ski-stick again. I held it with both hands and heaved, thrusting one foot on the front wall and one on the wall behind me. I jammed them hard and rested for a moment. Then I repeated the process – up a few inches, move my feet, up a few inches and rest a moment. Slowly I had climbed out to lie gratefully on the ice floe, my sopping wet clothes instantly transformed into rigid frozen boards.

Afterwards when Ran told that story, although not much changed, he seemed compelled – as with all tales of that expedition – to make out that I was far behind. Thus he had raced back hundreds of yards, retracing his tracks to find me. It was impossible. I'd have died if he hadn't been so close. He saw such exaggerations as harmless embellishment to an essentially accurate story. I, however, resented being made to appear weaker than in fact I was. I never heard him tell of how I had taken weight off his sledge to help him when his feet were bad and he was moving slowly. Now that he had been slower from the beginning of the expedition, I thought that even artistic licence would be unable to recreate the 'black dots'.

I was a contented man. As the sun shone down from deep blue skies I could even see beauty in the emptiness. It was all so vast and so untouched, and it was less cold and uncomfortable than on our Arctic trip. The days were generally non-threatening and life in the tent, warmed like a greenhouse by the relatively high sun, was truly sane. Even our clothing, iced from the day's perspiration, would dry overnight, whereas up north we had had frost in our sleeping bags. In the morning, as I unzipped the door to go outside, sunshine poured in and, although the air was cold, it was like opening a window after waking in the early spring. It was crisp, and I almost expected the birds to be singing. Later in the day, I found myself doing so. Within a few days we would reach land, and within four weeks the plateau. Then it would be only a month to the Pole. I was thinking positively.

Unfortunately, although I did try to regulate my pace, it just didn't work. It has been well documented by physiologists that a man performing a sustained task of any kind will subconsciously choose to work at his most efficient level. Generally this is at around thirty or forty per cent of the maximum that he could sustain for a short time, although someone highly trained might manage to keep up fifty per cent over an extended period. I began to get more frustrated. The only answer was to let me have part of his load. I understood his reluctance – it would certainly deliver another dent to his pride – but it was becoming a practical necessity.

On the evening of Day 18 we had our first serious disagreement and that led to a marked exacerbation of my frustration. Ehrling Kagge had begun his journey a few days behind us, and Ran and I discussed whether we should let him know our position. Ran was reluctant to do so, saying that he could find his own route, although he had already warned Kagge of the crevasse fields we had encountered. They would have been incredibly dangerous for a man on his own. This warning had led Kagge, to depart farther to the west than we had, with the obvious intention of staying on Berkner Island where it would be safer. However, instead of starting from the coast itself, he had asked to be dropped off at exactly the same latitude as we had started. At that longitude, his starting point was about ten miles in from the ice-edge. He had demonstrated that, for him, we rather than the Antarctic were the challenge. He had no understanding of the spirit in which these journeys should be made.

At the same time, whether or not Kagge saw it as a race, I had no qualms about letting him know our position. If we didn't provide the information we were likely to appear more competitive. Surely complete openness was the best approach, friendliness preferable to enmity. Finally Ran seemed to consent to this argument, but in the morning he had changed his mind. Instead of discussing it further, he came out with his first declaration of leadership.

'I have been thinking about what we discussed last night,' he announced, 'and I've decided that, although I'll tell Mo that you would wish her to transmit our positions to Kagge, I will also tell her – as expedition leader – that I believe it to be against the sponsors' interest. It would help Kagge by allowing him to pace himself, and by guiding him to the best route. It could definitely help him to beat us to the Pole.'

I couldn't believe it. I thought Ran was incredibly arrogant to make this declaration without further discussion. It seemed so unreasonable, and as for the patronising stuff about sponsors' interests – it was crap! He wasn't thinking about sponsors as much as his own competitive urges. He was going to see it as a race as long as he thought we might win – even if he knew that the chances were virtually nil. Yet I also knew from past experience that it was going to be hopeless to argue. I decided not to press the point. Later I would just make sure it was clear that I didn't wish to be so petty.

When we started out that day, it had been my intention to keep my anger under control. It was not as easy as I had imagined. Inside I was boiling with a fury far beyond anything warranted by the Kagge issue. I simmered all day, quite unable to forget it. It wasn't that I felt like having another argument about Kagge, I could see Ran's point of view even if I didn't agree with it; it was the leadership thing that I despised. There were just the two of us out here, facing the Antarctic together, as friends. How could one be leader?

I was so annoyed that I saw ill in everything Ran was doing. When, as for the last few days, he led too slowly, instead of relaxing behind him and accepting the pace, I thought of him as lazy. When he started to wander from side to side, not concentrating, instead of just letting it go I kept asking him to check the compass. When he stopped to adjust his uncomfortable harness, I thought he was stupid to be wearing it too loose and then complaining. I was very intolerant. On my leads I pushed hard, knowing that he was struggling to keep up and yet enjoying the fact. It was a mistake. Although he pressed himself and did maintain my speed when following, it made him even slower during his own turns in front. It came to a head when we stopped for our second soup. I had to say something.

'Are you all right?' I asked, as if concerned.

'Yes.' There was an edge to his voice as he clearly recognised what was coming.

'Then why are you going so bloody slowly and wandering from side to side? Can't you concentrate?'

Although I couldn't see them, I knew his fingers were clenched and that it took considerable self control for him not to explode. He couldn't hide the bitter anger in his voice when he replied.

'I'm going as fast as I can, and I don't expect some little runt to tell me it's too slow. It's bad enough anyway without being judged at the end of each hour, and it's your going too fast that's exhausting me. I'll go as slowly as I damn well like.'

I was not to be put off. I was fuming about his assertion of leadership and I didn't mind his anger or humiliation.

'It's not just that you are going slowly, Ran, you're weaving

75

from side to side and not following the shortest line. If you can't take the pace, we should do something about it. I really think I should take some of your load.'

'We can discuss that later,' he said. 'As you well know, I don't think that's necessary.'

We drank the remainder of the soup in strained silence and then moved off for our final two hours. I noticed that he kept up through mine, and then went fast through his. So, he *was* capable of moving faster. To my mind, this affirmed that his pace was, at least in part, a psychological reaction to his stupid fears about his age, rather than a strict physical limitation. He was so upset by finding things difficult that he was dwelling on it and making things worse. He just had to believe that he could still do it, pull his finger out and recognise that going slightly more slowly than a man ten years his junior was no big deal.

By the time it came to pitching camp our tempers were beginning to subside. I now recognised that I had been too harsh as a result of our disagreement over Kagge, and poor Ran didn't even realise that this was the reason for my aggressiveness. He must have wondered what had happened to his easy going partner. I apologised for my attack, and Ran accepted that and apologised for his speed. It had always been the same. If we did have differences of opinion, we were both sensible enough to push them away and not allow them to dominate the situation. A long-term breakdown in relations would make our journey impossible.

Yet, aggressive or not, my suggestion that I should start taking some of Ran's load remained reasonable. We would both get farther quicker if I did and I had to persuade him to agree. In my anxiety to do so, I made a stupid decision before broaching the subject again.

'Since we left, we've been able to eat only half the butter and breakfast cereal, and despite the heavy work, we haven't felt hungry. It seems to me that 5,300 calories a day is more than we need, and we can probably get away with 5,000 calories, as we did in the Arctic. We're about to hit the coast and to start climbing, so why don't we ditch the food we've saved so far, taking all the weight off your sledge.'

76

'What if we want to go on longer than a hundred days?' asked Ran.

'If we're not too hungry now, after nearly three weeks with the sledges at their heaviest, we shouldn't be too hungry later. To carry any unnecessary food as we begin to climb could be detrimental to our overall chances of success, and anyway, with our delayed departure, the ship will be leaving on Day 102, so there won't be much option for extending rations. It's really only a question of whether on the ration we're eating, we're ever likely to become hungry.'

'Well, I agree that it's unlikely to get too bad. The food so far has been more than adequate.'

I was quick to urge him on. 'Yes, and our speed's been better than we anticipated. Once we're up on the plateau we should be able to haul fifteen miles a day or more, and beyond the Pole, we'll get the wind. A hundred days actually looks feasible.'

'I'm not so sure about that, but since we probably can't get the ship to wait more than a couple of days, I suppose we might as well not carry more than is really necessary. We can always save a little later if we need to extend it. Let's do it.'

'And we'll take all the weight off your sledge?'

'Okay,' he replied. 'At least that way your load remains as it would have been anyway.'

I was delighted, and since it was becoming clear that in the warmer conditions of Antarctica, our fuel usage was lower than we had planned, we could also afford to ditch some fuel. This came off Ran's sledge too, and so immediately we achieved a reduction of twenty pounds or more. I have to admit that the food argument might have been less persuasive if I could have borne the thought of Ran going even more slowly up the hill. As for my prediction of not getting too hungry, I couldn't have been more wrong.

We reached land on Day 20. As we approached we were unable to tell the difference between ice-shelf and continent, but the pulling soon told us. Although the slope was virtually indiscernible, the work became much harder and changed from mere drudgery to bone-crushing toil. To add to the difficulties, the terrain became disrupted. We had reached the region where the winds poured down from the plateau and instead of the flat calm sea we were crossing an ocean caught in the midst of a storm. Windblown dunes formed a frozen mountainous swell, while on their crests, gale-carved sastrugi were petrified breaking waves. Each was caught at the very moment that it curled, and rank upon rank of these obstructions stood before us. We struggled through them, skis slipping, sledges catching, demoralised by this new and terrible effort.

Every day seemed the hardest yet. We climbed only to find that we lost most of the gain as we dropped into the next valley. We pulled through one region of storm-tossed ice to find that the next was worse. It was awful work, and I seemed much more affected than Ran. Whether this was due to his size giving him greater absolute pulling power; or whether his lighter sledge was helping, I don't know, but it was not long before I rued my decision to lighten his load. Within a couple of days we began to eat the food from my sledge with a view to making the weights even again.

Yet, despite the difficulties, our speed did increase to eleven or twelve miles a day and slowly we gained altitude. The increasing height would inevitably mean colder weather and stronger winds, but we wished for nothing more than to reach 6,000 feet, the point at which the slope to the Pole would become more gradual. Where was this point? We were unsure, and neither did we know if our route was free of mountains. Our maps were conflicting and unreliable. Charles Swithinbank had recommended that we travel up the thirty-nine degree west line of longitude, all the way from the Antarctic coast to the Pole. He had assured us that on that line, we would meet little in the way of crevassing and no mountains. However, nobody had actually travelled in the area before, and some of the maps we had conflicted with Swithinbank's opinion. They showed mountains lying close to thirty-nine degrees, and the map that had proved to be most accurate so far, appeared to show an ice-covered nunatak dead in our path. Ran christened this the 'Bogman' and it became our next goal.

The name Bogman, came from the origins of my surname, Anglo-Saxon for marsh dweller. It was a nickname that Ran had used for some years – I think in retaliation for my calling him the 'Frenchman'. I did this as a deliberate bait for his patriotic fervour, and to my endless amusement, he found it quite insulting. He even went to considerable lengths to explain that not only was his family documented to have lived in England for the last thousand years, but in any case their origins were Norman, and they were most certainly not 'French'! Either way, Anglo-Saxon myth or otherwise, the Bogman stood halfway to the Pole.

We had seen our first peak on Day 23, a small triangle of rock, far over to the west and, although it was difficult to judge the distance, it hardly changed over the next two or three days and certainly wasn't close. Eventually it dropped away below the horizon. A few days later, we saw a second mountain, which this time appeared to move steadily backwards during ten hours of hauling. It was also to our west but clearly much closer, and we estimated that it must be a peak of four or five thousand feet, ten or fifteen miles distant. It was unmarked on any of our maps, and although it didn't affect us in terms of route, it didn't give us much confidence in the cartography.

Finally, on Day 25, we passed the spot where the Bogman should have been situated. Charles Swithinbank was right – there was nothing. We rewarded ourselves in the only way we could, Ran generously giving me one of the King-size Mars bars which he carried for such occasions. He also ate one himself. We had half with our tea and the rest the following morning. We were now a quarter of the way through our journey and the plateau lay ahead. It should be easier going, and we were still happy with our progress. I had only one worry. We were now eating all of each day's rations, yet our relish for those Mars bars seemed abnormal. The climb was draining our reserves and we were very hungry.

SIX

★

In the Bleak Mid-Summer

IT IS THE PRIVILEGE of all Polar explorers to suffer from piles and Ran, being no exception to this edict, always took good care when it came to his morning ablutions. Up in the Arctic, this had meant performing in the tent, taking accurate advantage of a used ration bag to create a neat and fairly odourless package. For my sake he used to time this to coincide with my leaving the tent to perform outside, a harsh daily duty that I euphemistically referred to as the 'call of the wild'. I was obviously a mere Polar fledgling and didn't yet suffer with any problems at the tail end.

Since setting off in Antarctica, my daily timing had proved to be somewhat variable, and Ran was unable to synchronise with me. As it was not so cold as in the Arctic he generally felt able to take enough time and care out in the sunshine, and so he also would pop outside. Normally this was just before we packed up, while I swept the hoar frost from the inside of the tent. To keep out of any wind, he would always choose to go close in on the leeward side. Invariably this was also the side on which we had pitched the door, in order that overnight it didn't drift up with snow. I have to admit I found it pretty irritating to come out of the tent and have to pick my way carefully to avoid a pile of turds.

When it was cold, Ran still went outside, using the bag technique and demonstrating once again, his complete immunity to embarrassment. It made no difference whatever to him whether I was there or not. Mind you, on a few mornings, when high winds would have made going outside intolerable, I also went inside, although I found overcoming my natural

80

British reserve exceptionally difficult. In fact, on a couple of occasions, the potential embarrassment was enough to quash in me the need to go at all – a striking example of how cultural influences can overcome the most primitive of urges.

I should perhaps add that when it was cold, as long as you bared all quickly and settled with cheeks to the wind, it was not the private parts that were the limiting factor but the hands which got too cold. When it came to the job of cleaning up, one just could not use toilet paper with mitts on. However, whatever the wind and weather had to offer, we generally coped with this essential everyday activity in good humour.

Coping was all very well if the digestive system was working properly, but during the night of Day 30, I found myself in my sleeping bag getting increasingly desperate. Being cold, I was reluctant to get up, and when finally I was forced out of the bag, I was in something of a hurry. Getting out of a double sleeping bag with hoods and a protective outer bag involves opening a considerable number of draw-cords, zips and velcro fasteners. In the Arctic this had always been a worry, for a Polar bear could have attacked at night, and although we kept a gun in the middle of the tent, by the time either of us could have picked it up, we would have been mincemeat. Quite frequently during those Arctic journeys we heard the sound of footsteps in the snow.

'Ran, did you hear that?' I would whisper softly.

'Yes,' would come the equally soft reply.

'What do you think?'

'I don't ... Shh! There it is again.'

Slowly we would try to get our arms out of the bags while making no noise – impossible with velcro; it always sounds as if you're ripping open a kettle drum.

'Where's the gun?' Inevitably it would be lost.

'It *was* in the middle. Isn't that it, under the pee bottle?'

One of us would pick it up while the other reached for the door zip – not that a Polar bear would observe such niceties as approaching from the door. We would open it slowly.

'I can't see anything. Perhaps it's gone.'

'No. I can still hear it ... It's somewhere over that side.'

'I'll throw some matches out. Okay?'

On expeditions we used lifeboat matches which can't be blown out and which light when wet. They also produce a pungent chemical smoke which, when we lit the stove at the end of each day, Ran and I used to welcome. At least it made a change from nothing. However, we had convinced ourselves that bears wouldn't like it and so used them as a repellent.

Several matches would be lit and thrown out in quick succession. Then there would be more tense listening.

'It's going away. They are definitely getting quieter.'

Eventually we would settle down again but would be unable to sleep for the rest of the night. In the morning, I would go out to the loo, armed with our pistol, but Magnum force was never needed. Not once did I ever find footprints to confirm our night-time paranoia.

Now, however, my need to escape from the bags had a different sense of urgency. It is extraordinary how easily one can control the most basic bodily function up to the point at which you have to do something about it. At that stage, there is a sudden change of gear in the urgency drive, and suddenly you are desperate, fighting to retain control while making the necessary preparations and keeping your legs crossed. It was a race to get out through the zips and velcro, to grab an empty ration bag and to squat in the corner of the tent. I won the race, but in my hurry failed to make the all important check. The ration bag was ripped open at both ends, and with near liquid diarrhoea it does not take much imagination to realise the consequences.

Fortunately the cause of the diarrhoea was not a stomach upset in the normal infective sense, but the fact that for two days I had been taking antibiotics and they had eliminated the gut bugs that are essential for normal function. These bugs are also the ones which usually make things so smelly, and with them gone, the diarrhoea was nearly odourless. The whole episode might have been a lot worse, and although it was not much fun clearing up, at least Ran remained asleep throughout and spared my blushes.

Through the remainder of the night I had several other urgent calls, wisely leaving the tent on each occasion, and by the morning, although I felt reasonably well, I was pretty drained. When we started pulling I found that I was far too weak, and the feeling was reinforced each time I had to stop and urgently squat down by my sledge, struggling with the over-shoulder straps of my salopettes and having to half undress and get very cold in the process. It was only at the very end of the trip that I worked out what the two zips down either side of the salopettes were for – they constituted a bum flap, but I wasn't bright enough to realise it.

Eventually enough was enough and I called Ran and told him that I had to stop. We had completed only three hours of our day, but I felt too ill to go on. We put up the tent and made some tea. I took some Immodium tablets to settle things down and tried to doze. These worked a treat, and after three or four hours, I was feeling much better. I got up and we carried on, but the improvement didn't last, and after a total of seven hours we had to stop again. Still, it wasn't bad for a day of illness.

I knew that a difficult decision had to be faced. I had started the antibiotics when I had first noticed a pain in my heel and, on removing my socks and boots, had found the beginnings of an infected abscess over my Achilles tendon. At the time it had seemed to contain no pus, and I hoped that by catching it early it would die down without trouble. The treatment had worked to an extent, and it had died down, but there was still a red and tender area remaining. I was pretty sure that if I stopped the tablets the abscess would develop rapidly. It might then spread to the tissues alongside the Achilles tendon, a problem that would be a real show-stopper.

Nevertheless, with the antibiotics giving me diarrhoea, I couldn't really continue to take them, and the only answer was to open the abscess and drain any poison inside. Taking a syringe of local anaesthetic, I gingerly injected the area, an unpleasant procedure at the best of times and made worse by the fact that the boots' rubbing for the last few weeks had made the skin as tough as leather. The needle could barely penetrate it, yet it seemed to have lost none of its sensitivity. It made my eyes water.

Once I had the anaesthetic in, I thought the worst would

be over, but I was wrong. When I took a scalpel and made a deep stab, the pain shot through my heel like a bolt. The agony was only brief, and then there was immediate relief as thick pus oozed from the wound, but to drain it properly I had to make a second cross-cut which was just as bad as the first. It was a particularly nasty experience. I certainly wouldn't recommend self-incision to others.

The procedure worked and the abscess improved from that moment on. After a couple of days it gave me no further trouble, and the diarrhoea also cleared up. But another episode later in the trip was to have rather more serious consequences.

On the day following my lancing operation, we woke up to a shaking, vibrating tent, keeled over hard in a south-easterly gale. With a windchill of around minus sixty, it was frightfully cold and in normal circumstances such conditions would have precluded travel. They would create a danger of frostbite and also the possibility that we might not be able to re-erect the tent. Worst of all, we could become separated in the wind-blown whiteout, which, with only one tent, would probably be fatal.

Our situation was anything but normal. Both our time and supplies were strictly limited. We prepared for departure as usual – except when it came to collapsing the tent. Then I stayed inside, spread-eagled on the floor, while Ran tried to gain control of the wildly bucking beast. Gusts of wind caught it like a sail and lifted us both bodily. In the end, Ran was able to wrestle it, bit by bit, into its bag while I slowly crawled out of the collapsed front door.

Once packed, we set off, staying close to one another in conditions that were simply appalling. The icy wind came blasting into our faces, no whetted knife, but a blunt instrument that bludgeoned our bodies and pummelled us with its savage uproar. I could see almost nothing, and white ground met white air and white sky with no delineation. There was neither contour nor contrast to provide information to the senses, and without them there was neither up nor down, just disorientation. When leading, I found myself making tight left-handed circles. I tried to walk without my hood or glasses, to see if I could pick up ground features as a guide, but although no hood allowed me to fix more easily on the direction of the wind, and hence walk in a straighter line, I could still see nothing. With the air thick with blowing snow and ice, I found that keeping my eyes uncovered was impossible. I also found that, with the hood down, the total whiteness was very disturbing, and I much preferred to have the blank view at least surrounded by a circle of fur. Through that circle, there still poured myriads of ice crystals that stung my face like enraged insects, but the brain was registering something, even if it was a circular television, after the close-down.

Ran proved somewhat better than I at maintaining his direction with no clues, and so for much of the time I followed him, fixating on the back of his sledge and walking on automatic pilot. Of course, whoever was leading stumbled and fell quite frequently, finding the obstacles by literally running into them. The whole experience was very frustrating, but although quite mad, it was also exciting and, strangely, did not feel threatening. Lost within the all encompassing whiteness, one could have been anywhere, and the millions of square miles of Antarctica – an expanse which normally made one feel so small – was reduced to an immediacy more akin to a mountainside in North Wales or Scotland. Although the weather was worse than any I had ever been out in, the day felt just like those I had spent walking through blizzards much closer to home.

It even went quite well, and that evening, after successfully completing our gamble and pitching the tent unscathed, we felt immodestly satisfied. Despite the difficulties, we had made reasonable progress and had not lost the day to the storm. Our sense of comradeship, one of the great pleasures of a trip such as ours, had never been greater. All the same, it had been very cold, and Ran had acquired some nasty frost injuries.

'My foot doesn't feel too good,' he murmured as he took off his boots and socks. 'I think the graft has gone again.'

'Let's have a look,' I said. 'Hold it up a bit.'

When we had returned home after the first expedition, Ran's frostbitten feet had been grafted but, even so, the area had always been vulnerable and had given trouble again on the last North Pole trip. Now it had broken down once more, either rubbed off or more likely frozen and then thawed. The skin beside the little toe on the right foot, was a pallid, soggy mess.

'It's the same problem all right,' I said, 'and it's going to rub like hell. In all likelihood it will become infected.'

I was right this time. The damaged area was soon to become a deep raw ulcer, abrading constantly on his boot. From that day until well beyond the end of the expedition, it would be a source of almost constant pain. Although a doctor, I had my own hardships and discomforts and could feel little true compassion. Ran was alone in his suffering, and a lesser man would have folded rapidly.

The storm continued unabated on the day following and the next, and on each we fought our way through, proud of our achievements. Then on the fourth day of the storm, the wind moved round to the north and was no longer in our faces. When we started that morning, visibility was still down to a few yards. For an hour or more, we stumbled along, going quite steeply downhill, but then we bottomed out and began to climb. Although it was difficult to discern in the mist, we soon realised that this hill was different, far steeper than any we had yet faced. As the gradient increased, the surface changed to grey ice and it became impossibly slippery. We were forced to start traversing, and this made the sledges slew round to the downhill side. As they did so, they twisted us and pulled us off our feet. It was desperately difficult, and after half an hour of the struggle we had had enough. We were prepared to try anything, and anything was using the sails in a whiteout.

We got them out and, with some difficulty in the strong wind, made ready. Then, with a flick on a riser, we were off, moving fast, and straight up the hill. All went reasonably well until we reached the top and flatter terrain. There we started to pick up immoderate speed, and it became absurdly dangerous to continue. Sastrugi rushed out of the mist and we had no time to avoid them. Dips caught us unawares and we took fall after fall. No doubt we also took risks with crevasses, but there was still that same intoxicating thrill we had noticed the first time – and every yard gained was a yard less to haul.

10 Operating the 'Up-ski' parachute sail

11 Mike manhauling across small sastrugi

12 Ran cutting his boot open to relieve the pressure on his foot

13 The plateau became a mental
as well as a physical problem

14 Mike playing chess
with urine samples

15 Ran with tea and a biscuit at the end of the day – life seems rosy

After forty-five minutes Ran suddenly shouted: 'Mike, you've dropped something.'

I glanced down at my sledge. Everything was done up as it should be but, looking back, I could see a small, dark object about a hundred yards behind.

'I can't have. Are you sure it isn't yours?'

'It's in your tracks,' he yelled above the wind.

Whatever could it be? I left my sledge and walked back. There in the snow lay the spare battery from the satellite beacon, and it slowly dawned on me that it must have come from inside the sledge, but how? I found the answer soon enough when I returned to examine the sledge.

'There's a bloody great big hole in it,' I told Ran. 'It's broken right open where it was flexing after the crevasse damage. We'll have to stop and do something.'

Ran made camp while I unloaded. Then we pulled the front half of the sledge in through the tent door.

'God, it's worse than I thought,' I muttered. 'The two halves are only held together by the runners and the cover.'

'We'll have to repair it somehow,' said Ran. 'There isn't any way of getting both loads on one sledge.'

It was true. It wasn't the weight, so much as the sheer volume. We still needed the room provided by two full hulls.

'Well, it can't be repaired,' I said slowly, 'but if we move some of the runner screws from the front and back to where they're missing by the break, it should help a little.'

On either side of the crack, where there had been a lot of movement, the screws that held the runners had popped out. If we managed to replace them, the runners would hold the crack together better.

'Cut slots on either side, and then tie them through with paracord to reinforce it,' Ran suggested.

It took a couple of hours and in the end the whole thing looked rather Heath Robinson, but the runners were tight. I had used straps off my rucksack to secure the slots tightly. It didn't look as if it would last for long, but if it would just hold together for a few more weeks, we would be all right. There was one more change to make. Even with the break narrowed, it was clear that the rear half would act like a scoop, picking up snow and rapidly increasing the load. To minimise this, and to reduce the strain on the join, the rope traces needed to be reversed, to put the bigger half of the sledge at the front. As I was changing them, I remembered a conversation I'd had with Graham Goldsmith, the manager of Gaybo, who had made the sledges for us.

The design was based on that used by the Footsteps of Scott expedition, but since we needed more room, we had asked Graham to make the sledges longer, and while he was at it to make each end a 'front'. This would allow us to reverse them if damage occurred. He had phoned me one day to ask if this was really important; he said it made the moulding more difficult and the sledge heavier. In his opinion the carbon fibre/Kevlar composite was virtually unbreakable and our concern about possible damage unwarranted. I had dithered, and said that I would get back to him. I discussed it with Ran. Fortunately he had entertained no such indecisiveness. He pointed out that it wasn't wear and tear that was likely to break a sledge but the possibility of a crevasse accident. In his opinion, we had to have the sledges double-ended. Circumstances proved him right.

With the sledge reversed, I packed the front half with all the heavier items and left the larger volume light stuff for the rear. Inevitably this was to make the sledge difficult to pull since the front became reluctant to rise over obstacles or to turn corners. The back half would sometimes scrape along the snow, acting as a partial brake and scooping up considerable quantities. Every night from that time on, once we had made camp, I had to shovel it out, and sometimes I had acquired several pounds of this unwanted extra baggage. Still, although articulated, at least the sledge could still carry a full load.

By the time we were finished it was almost five o'clock. The wind had died and it was a rather dull and unattractive evening. My feelings were to give up for the day on the grounds that another couple of hours just weren't worth it. Ran had other ideas. He insisted that we should set off again and try to complete four hours in order to achieve at least ten miles, the absolute minimum daily mileage if we were to reach the Pole in time to have any chance of completing our journey.

On the plateau, our speeds had been disappointing, and we had been forced to moderate our plateau aim of fifteen miles a day to a more realistic target. The slowness was due to a continuation of undulating ground and therefore more climbing than we had anticipated. The temperatures were also much lower now. The cold made the surfaces sticky. Snow is only slippery if downward pressure can melt a thin layer of water under the runners or skis. In the extreme cold this doesn't happen, and the snow becomes no more slippery than sand. In fact, it can be worse. At least sand grains are rounded, whereas snow crystals are covered in those beautiful microscopic spicules that stick to each other. The result is a substance about as slippery as soft cement. The sledges seemed heavier than when we had started, and even on flattish terrain, the pulling was nothing like it had been back on the ice-shelf. I certainly wasn't singing.

Reluctantly I helped Ran to take down the tent and, with my lip thick with resentment, I donned my harness and followed him into the gloom. In the event we pulled for four and a half hours more, making about twelve miles, and afterwards I was glad that Ran had pushed me into it. Beyond doubt, this was one of his great strengths. He was always determined to meet his target and never allowed himself to take the easy way out. Although I might have had a slight physical advantage, he had the greater determination, and I always depended upon him for motivation. I have to admit that, in this sense, he was the leader.

Even twelve miles was no great achievement. That evening, while we relaxed with the blissful first tea and flapjack, Ran made a new suggestion.

'Mike, I've been thinking...'

'What?'

'We're just not making the pace we need. So I've worked out a new schedule. If we start saving food now, just small amounts out of every meal, we should be able to last for more than a hundred and twenty days. That would still give us a reasonable chance even at ten miles a day to the Pole and no more than twelve miles a day over the rest of the plateau.'

I glanced at him. He was looking at columns of figures in his diary and had a satisfied smile on his face. I was simply horrified. Lasting a hundred days with reasonable food was the limit of my nightmare. The prospect of making it even longer didn't bear thinking about. Anyway, I couldn't agree with Ran that we could walk while eating less. Saving food now would be no advantage.

'It won't work,' I said. 'Don't you remember how bad things became at the end of the Siberia trip?'

In the days leading up to the finish, we had become progressively slower and slower, and our rucksacks, which weighed only 40lbs, had crushed us as if they were the world. After our pick-up, and the week's stay on the Russian drift station, we had returned to our base camp where Paul Cleary, once again our film director, had wanted footage of us carrying the packs instead of hauling. We had gone out to some open snow-covered country and put on precisely the same loads as we had borne a week before. They weighed almost nothing. They were peanuts for men in any reasonable condition, but for us they had been like lead weights. I hadn't forgotten the lesson. I didn't want to repeat it.

'If we eat more now,' I went on, 'we'll retain our strength for longer. *And* the sledges will become lighter, faster. If we do as you suggest, even saving only a couple of ounces of food a day, it will mean that we burn an extra couple of ounces from our body stores. Every week we would lose an extra pound of body weight, an extra pound that will be left on our sledges. By the Pole, we'd be finished.'

'Well, we can leave it for a while if you like,' he said airily, 'but I reckon that if we take off tiny amounts now, we won't even notice them. Later we'll be glad of it.'

Over the next couple of nights we had the same conversation, and Ran finally brought me round to his way of thinking. With our slow progress on the plateau, the journey was beginning to look impossible in a hundred days. Hence we might as well try to save food now. On Day 33, I started to take small quantities from each of our freeze-dried meals and at the same time we both ate a square or two of chocolate less each day. We began to create a hoard for the future, but it made us curse our ditching the food two weeks before.

Our resolution lasted four days. On Day 37, we camped on a surface that was firm enough to give us an accurate body weight measurement. It was the first for the last couple of weeks. We were carrying miniature scales, as part of our scientific programme, but they were near useless unless we were camped on ice. Now they gave us the unwelcome news. We had both lost nearly twenty pounds and, along with measurements showing big decreases in our waist and neck circumferences, it was clear that we were eating inadequately. At that rate of loss, let alone faster, we would disappear completely before our hundred days were up. The climb was sapping us of everything we had, and there was no choice but to return to eating full rations.

As the second month progressed we finally began to encounter flatter surfaces and, although they were still like cement, I began to pull ahead. Once more I became frustrated by Ran's polar plod. It was now slower still, and when following, I had to stop intermittently to let him get a little distance in front. When I led, I invariably left him behind, and although I appreciated that this was not good for his morale and made efforts to slow down, I couldn't change my pace. Generally, at the end of my session of leading, I would sit and wait on the sledge, and to put things in perspective, he was never more than five or ten minutes behind. However, just as before, when he did catch up, his reactions would be mixed. More often he said nothing, or apologised for being slow; on some occasions he was very angry.

'I suppose you're feeling proud of yourself after that fucking display.'

I was just getting to my feet after sitting and waiting for a few minutes. Ran was shaking with fury.

'What do you mean,' I said slowly.

'You just want to rub it in. To bloody well show off. But the effort will burn you up.'

It was unlike Ran to swear; in fact it was most unusual, and I was taken aback. I felt confused, a mixture of embarrassment and anger. The anger won out. What on earth made him think that I could be bothered to show off.

'Don't be so pathetic. I never whinged when you were out in the front in the Arctic. Pride and showing off are your problem not mine.'

'The Arctic wasn't the same,' he retorted. 'There it was of value if I went out in front and scouted the route. It saved you from wasting your time. Here, your disappearing ahead is just demoralising.'

There was some truth in what he said. Out in the Arctic, when he did get ahead, he would stop and leave his sledge to seek the best route through the ice-pressure. In the end it did save some time. Nevertheless my morale had suffered during those early days when I trailed and I had never complained. I had only apologised for holding him up, and he was in no position to be too critical now.

'Well, like it or not, pointless or not, I don't do it deliberately. All men work at a pace that suits themselves, and it is difficult to modify it. I've tried to slow down for you but I can't, and in any case I don't go so fast that you couldn't keep up with a bit more effort. If you weren't so convinced you were past it and had to take it easy, you'd have no trouble.'

Ran suddenly looked bowed and sad, and I saw his anger draining away.

'Sorry,' he muttered, 'I know I'm going slowly. But I am too old for this and, as I said before, I shouldn't have come on this expedition. But you are going too fast. You'll burn yourself out.'

I felt mean for being so angry. 'I'm sorry too,' I said. 'I know it must be difficult for you, but you're not really that much slower, and it's your pride that's the problem. We're still faster than Footsteps of Scott – or Messner.'

It was true – and with our vastly greater loads. Our daily mileage was better than any of the manhauling expeditions that had headed for the Pole before us. We put in longer hours and we had no rest days. It was ridiculous of Ran to think he wasn't up to it, and by so doing he was making himself feel down, which slowed him even more.

'Just don't worry about it,' I continued. 'We're doing pretty well, and although I can't make myself walk more slowly, I'm happy to take weight off you again if you want.'

We sat down on the sledges and drank our soup together, and in those minutes the wall we had built between us fell. Each of us preferred conciliation to confrontation, and by the time the cups were empty, our disagreement was virtually forgotten. Being logical, we accepted one another's arguments. I would start taking extra weight off Ran's sledge again and would also try to control my speed. We knew that the same problem would arise again in the days ahead, but we thought we could cope with it. Whatever happened, I knew that our relationship would remain strong. I didn't reckon on an event to come a couple of weeks later.

As Christmas approached we made our pulling hours longer and longer in an attempt to get our distances up to thirteen or fourteen miles. Then we had our first bit of luck.

On 23rd December we had a little wind at the end of the day and, using our sails, travelled until after 9 p.m., pushing up our distance to more than thirteen miles in twelve hours. Very cold and tired, we stopped, put up the tent and had a meal. At midnight, with the wind persisting, we set off again. It was beautiful. Normally we travelled in the local daytime, with the sun moving round behind us, allowing us to use the time and our shadows as a guide to our heading. It also minimised the risks to our eyes. Now we were sailing towards the sun, effortlessly sweeping over a smooth surface, with the warmth on our faces. It felt like heaven and anything seemed possible. We would sail to the Pole, traversing in a couple of days what otherwise would take several weeks. Of course our optimism was unfounded. The wind died after a little more than an hour and by 2 a.m. we were in our bags and back to the prospect of hauling.

The next morning, Christmas Eve, we set off in gloomy conditions. There was a mocking wind from the north-east that had us trying to sail twice before 9 a.m. Each time it proved just not strong enough and all that happened was time wasted rigging the chutes and then putting them away again. We became very cold. Then, at around ten o'clock, the wind began to rise once more, and although after our earlier disappointments we were reluctant to take advantage of it, it persistently blew on our hoods as we moved along and eventually nagged us into trying again. At first it barely moved us. Slowly we veered off in the wrong direction, for you could only sail at an angle to the wind if it had enough strength. That soon changed. The wind grew and spindrift began to hiss around us. As our speed increased we began to surge along, carried by the rising tide. Before we knew it, we were racing, flashing over a range of surfaces, fighting for control in the diminishing visibility. Every so often huge belts of sastrugi crossed our path, walls of ice up to four feet high combined with dunes and pits to create effective mantraps. We did our best to avoid them, but had many accidents, and the chutes got tangled on the many obstructions. This often caused an inversion, where the canopy turned completely inside out. In the strong wind it was very difficult to correct, and even when the chute was right-side out, the lines were invariably tangled. We could only sort them out by releasing them at their origin, the control box, and then carefully follow the lines forward, undoing knots one by one. It could only be done with gloves off, and several times I noticed my fingers turning white, solid and numb. The cold was causing damage but the wind had come at last.

After three hours, when I stopped with yet another inverted chute, we decided to have some soup. We sat down together and drank it quickly. The cold was almost intolerable, and we knew that when we started again we would get little respite. Unlike manhauling, the sailing, although strenuous, didn't generate continuous heat. It tended to keep you out of the wind by allowing you to ride with it, but you couldn't warm up after any stops. It was exciting and thrilling to make good progress, but it was at a cost. We were bruised and cold and knew that we were taking risks.

The soup finished, I went back over to untangle the sail, detaching the control box from the sledge to do so. As I picked up the box an especially strong gust caught the leading edge of the canopy. It unhooked from the sastrugus it was caught

94

on and instantly inflated. The control line for the centre hole was released and inflation should have been impossible, but the line was caught in the tangled shrouds and friction prevented it from running freely. The centre hole was effectively held closed, and with the box disconnected, the pull was entirely on me. The chute could generate up to a thousand pounds of pull, and the wind was now strong enough to apply that sort of force. I was ripped from my feet and dragged forward.

I hung on for dear life. I couldn't let it go or the sail might disappear for ever. I was dragged through pits and smashed against ice obstacles, first on my front and then on my back. I must have been doing twenty miles an hour. Snow packed into my mouth and went down my neck and in my gloves, but I hung on grimly, desperately trying to release one of the emergency toggles, the release that would allow the lines on one side of the chute to break away completely.

I just couldn't reach it. When pulled over, I was holding on with one hand and banging over the ice. I had to use the other arm to protect my head. I needed a smooth section for long enough to get my hand to the toggle. For several hundred yards this didn't happen and I could feel my grip getting weaker. I wouldn't be able to hold on much longer. My fingers were uncurling from the cords. Then I had a chance. As I flew off the top of a large rise, I saw about fifty yards of open ice ahead before a big hole filled with blue ice walls. It was going to be the last opportunity, I could never hold on through that. I reached up with the flailing arm and tried to pull the emergency release. Cold fingers refused to cooperate. The pit rushed nearer. There were only a couple of seconds left as I tried again, my hand a simple claw. It caught and mercifully the shrouds released.

I lay face down, pummelled but triumphant. After a moment, I got to my feet and walked slowly back to the sledges.

'Interesting technique,' Ran said, 'but I don't think it will catch on.'

'No,' I said, in as offhand a way as I could. 'I think I'll give it a miss in future.'

After untangling the chute – this time attached to the sledge – we were off again. Although the wind was still from the wrong direction, and we could do no better than head south-west, we finally got in over eight hours of sailing. At the end of the day we had gone twenty-four miles south, and a similar distance to the west, but that didn't matter. We journeyed to the point where all lines of longitude would meet, and although we were cold and stiff, we were thrilled. A whole day's hauling had been saved, and we had received the best Christmas present we could hope for. A bit early perhaps, but maybe we would get more the next day.

'Merry Christmas.' Ran's greeting permeated through to my consciousness and reluctantly I gave up my wide-ranging dream and came back to our limited world. 'Coffee's ready.'

'Thanks ... What time is it?'

'Only six, but the wind's still blowing.'

I sat up stiffly. It felt as if I had had a disagreement with Mike Tyson. I was bruised everywhere from the previous day's fun-ride and the discomfort was to persist for the best part of a week.

'Right,' I said. 'Let's go.'

By 7.30 we were off again with the wind pulling us swiftly. I really thought 'this is it'. I wanted the help so much. I saw another twenty or thirty miles to be had that day. Who knows, it might go on blowing and carry us all the way to the Pole. I was wrong.

It wasn't that the wind died, but it blew in the wrong direction. After only a few minutes, I noticed that however hard I tried to pull to the left, our shadows still looked wrong. At that time in the morning, with the sun in the east, the shadows should have been out at ninety degrees. It was the way we ran our day. As a rule, we set off with them to our right and travelled until they lay to the left. Now, although we still seemed to be crossing the sastrugi, which for the past few days had always crossed our path from east to west, our shadows ran in front of us. We were heading very little south of west, and the compass confirmed it.

There was nothing for it but to take down the chutes and resume our manhauling. To have gone on with the wind would have been pointless. Its direction must have changed in the night, and the prevailing wind which had carved the sastrugi in this region, was clearly somewhat different to the one behind us. It was bitterly disappointing. After starting off believing we would do so well, we were now back to our pitifully slow progress, crawling across the vastness, the Pole as far away as ever.

The day was bloody awful, the worst we had had by far, and no way in which to spend Christmas. The icy wind blew harder and harder across our path, and I wanted nothing else but to give up. To make matters worse, we soon hit a hill so steep that we could have been back at the beginning of our ascent. In ever decreasing visibility, we dragged our virtually immovable loads up the merciless slope. We were back to needing rest stops, unable to maintain the crushing effort. To compound the matter, Ran also developed a mild stomach upset and twice had to stop in the howling wind to answer a dreadful call.

For the whole day it continued. Although the first hill was the worst, it was followed by several others, with short steep downhill sections between each, sections that provided only brief respite. We gradually became exhausted. I tried to think of my family on Christmas morning, opening presents, the children so happy, but it was too difficult. It was just too far from our experience of the moment and Mo had had no messages to pass from home for the last few days. I didn't know where they were and so I couldn't place them. For moments I could push my mind to our cottage last year, I could see the tree and the lights and the star, but my family wasn't there and I didn't know where to look.

At lunchtime we stopped briefly. 'Where's Ginny at the moment?' I asked.

'With family and friends,' Ran answered. 'What about Thea and the children?'

'I don't know,' I said miserably. 'Holland, my father's, my mother's, I haven't a clue. Mind you, I know one thing for sure. Their lunch is better than this.'

Just a flicker of a smile crossed Ran's face. Back home, everyone would be sitting round a big table, facing the turkey with all the trimmings, wine in hand, heating on. In brutal contrast, we sat huddled together on Ran's sledge, hunched against the blasting wind. Vainly we sought warmth in our proximity, but the cold pushed fingers through our clothing and ice formed right against our skin. Spindrift stung our eyes and faces while in chilled hands we held our mugs of cold and fatty soup. On our knees there rested three small squares of chocolate. Ahead was nothing but white, bleak, emptiness. It was the most miserable moment of our journey. And it was unbelievably lonely.

Things were no better by the end of the day. We didn't even achieve our ten miles. Ran gave me a Christmas present of another kingsize Mars bar, but it made me feel bad that I hadn't been so thoughtful as to bring something like it for him. It would have been so easy to have been carrying a 'goodie', but it had never occurred to me. After we ate, we turned on the radio and called up Mo, anticipating Christmas messages from home. Now, we were to hear what we had been looking forward to so much.

The tape started, first with words from Thea, then it faded and we heard nothing. Our families seemed further away than ever, and our tent was a tiny spot in the middle of a vast frozen wasteland.

SEVEN

★

Calling the Shots

I N THE PERIOD between Christmas and the New Year we struggled on, making low mileages each day. On Boxing Day, Mo relayed messages from home, but instead of lifting my spirits, they served to depress me further. Callan 'loved his daddy', but he wanted a *Tracy Island* and wondered when I could make him one. Tarn said 'pull hard, pull together' but it was not encouragement aimed at Ran and me; it was just a quote from *Thomas the Tank Engine*. They were both too young to understand why Daddy wasn't home, and although Thea was as strong as ever, she deserved better – a husband that did his share.

If anything, we were even slower than before. I continued to find the work easier than Ran but my morale was falling faster. His mental approach was better, and he seemed able to focus on the Pole as his objective, and to ignore the second half of the journey. While I saw things slipping away, he saw only a couple of hundred miles to go.

On the last evening of 1992, following a day in which we had both felt physically drained, we set up camp once more on a surface that was firm enough to weigh ourselves – the first opportunity since that time on Day 37. The return to full rations had done little to help. Ran had now lost forty pounds, and I more than thirty. We must have been burning more than 8,000 calories a day while eating just over 5,000. This meant a deficit of nearly 3,000 calories every day, the equivalent in normal terms of being on a starvation diet in which one stopped eating altogether. It was no wonder that we were feeling so rough.

When you are hungry, your body starts to live off its fat stores and, as a product of their metabolism, makes chemicals called ketones. These circulate in the blood, and make you feel generally unwell and depressed. Our diet was already high in fat, which probably made the problem worse. It was pretty obvious that we had to start eating more if we were to reach the Pole in any state to go on. At the same time, it was a big step to start eating into food for the second half of the expedition, and we were both reluctant to take it.

On New Year's Day, at the end of the third hour, Ran came up slowly and we sat down together for a drink. He was even quieter than usual. Suddenly, he turned to me.

'Mike, I can no longer hack it. I've been struggling since Day 37, and I just can't go on like this.'

I caught my breath. Had he just said what I thought he did? Was this it – were we about to give up? What did I think? On the one hand I was thrilled – all the pain would be over – but on the other it seemed crazy. The expedition might yet be successful. We could at least make it to the Pole.

Ran continued. 'I'm sorry but we've got to do something about it. I've decided that the Polar plod will have to be slower still.'

I breathed again. So he wasn't thinking of giving up, just going more slowly. It was a strange way to put it. 'Well, you have to go at whatever pace you can,' I said, 'but you know as well as I do, that we're just not eating enough. Perhaps the answer is to eat more now and less later.'

'I don't know,' he murmured. 'I just don't know.'

We left it at that for the moment and carried on pulling. Through that day I began to come to terms with failure. It seemed to me that we could make the Pole but probably not much farther. We were becoming weaker by the day, and by the time we reached the Pole we would be wasted. There was only one thing to be done: we had to eat more now to regain some strength.

That evening, after a lot of discussion, we made the decision. We would eat six extra rations over the couple of weeks before the Pole, and then plan to compensate by using half rations from Day 84 onwards. It would still give us a range of more than 110 days, and although the days after 84 would be difficult, with luck we would be off the plateau and heading down the Beardmore Glacier. Sledges would be light, there might be following winds, and our first goal, the far side of the continent, would be very close. By then optimism should be back to support us, and if everything went favourably, we might still cross the Ross ice-shelf to Scott Base. Furthermore, we wouldn't consume all the extra rations – only the breakfast cereal, butter and evening meal, and so the half rations would still have a full quota of chocolate, soup and flapjacks. We also decided to lighten further Ran's load, and to take five consecutive rations off his sledge, and since we were still going well on the fuel front, we could take a couple of bottles off as well.

Ran was immediately much brighter. His whole demeanour changed and I realised that things had been oppressing him more than I had thought. Suddenly he was the jovial man with whom I had set out, a character that I had almost forgotten. He began to talk of the expedition beyond the Pole and seemed full of optimism about the final outcome. I didn't feel so confident. It seemed to me that the chances of success were diminishing by the moment, and I knew that, even riding on Ran's determination, I needed to feel there was a reasonable chance of finally making it. I'm not the sort of person who can press on for the hell of it and I began to fear that in the end it would be I who couldn't hack it . . .

As New Year passed the fields of cement continued and the enormity of our undertaking struck deeper and deeper into my heart. I became ever more disillusioned and could no longer escape into day-dreams. Everything I had turned over in my head earlier in the trip was gone. It was as if I had thought things through so many times that now there was nothing left. I was becoming locked into circular thoughts of the expedition and the rest of my mind was empty, echoing the awful place we crossed. Desperately I tried to escape the purgatory but could see little point in our being here. Of course, there was the fund-raising for multiple sclerosis; at least that was worthwhile. I had worked for six months at the National Hospital for Neurology and so knew the condition well. I had seen patients who struggled harder than we did now for every day of their lives, trying with all their will to maintain their mobility and independence. What were our difficulties and suffering when compared with theirs? The answer was that ours were nothing, but it didn't help me. Increasingly, the whole concept of the expedition, any expedition, seemed so ridiculous that even charity was not enough to dispel the depression that came to dominate large parts of the day, and I began to consider any means of escape from going on. I recognised these black moods, and they carried with them unwelcome memories.

I was back again in the Arctic. Ran was far ahead. The pack ice was broken and we were crossing pressure ridges every few yards. I couldn't see him, and hadn't done so for the last couple of hours. I just followed his track as it wove a tortuous path through and over the obstacles. My hands were frostbitten, swollen in my gloves, and my feet were a blistered, bleeding mess. They ground against my boots as I stumbled on my way, and my whole body cried out for relief from this ridiculous effort. I hated him. There was no other word for it. Why couldn't he help instead of disappearing into the distance? It was fatuous that I should be left behind, trying to follow and pulling the same load. He weighed nearly half as much as me again and should have taken his fair share based on that. The sledge got stuck again, jammed hard under another ice block. I turned to free it but fell on a loose ice boulder. It must have been the twentieth time that morning that I'd crashed down hard. I swore. I would show him! He thought I was easy going and would just accept it all. Well, I wouldn't. He should have known that such loads were impossible on pack ice and we should never have tried it. I was bloody well not going to be doing this for weeks for his benefit, and neither was I going to give up and return in shame.

An accident – that's what is needed. Preferably one that injures him and not me, but how? The gun – that's the answer. I carried it in my sledge and had it in the tent at night. It could easily go off by mistake – but could it? If it went off in the tent and I shot Ran in the leg or foot, he might see that it was deliberate. No, it was better actually to shoot him, and get rid of the body in the sea. Nobody would ever find him. I could tell the world of the Polar bear, the frozen gun, and the end of one of the greatest travellers who had ever lived. It would even mean fame instead of shame, and it was really all his fault.

He was coming back. As I crossed a ridge, I saw his figure about a hundred yards away. He would be bringing the soup – he got too cold if he waited for me to come up and so he walked back with it. We must have completed five hours. Thank God! Nearly half the day over and I could have a brief rest. Afterwards I would feel better. It had been the same each day since starting.

'How's it going?' Ran asked as he appeared just ahead.

'Fine,' I replied. 'I'm sorry, I can't go any faster.'

'That's all right, we're doing pretty well really, and I don't mind waiting, but I can't go any slower than I am. That's just the pace I'm used to.'

We would drink the soup together and then he would walk back into the distance, not to be seen again until the next break. Sometimes he would help me to pull up my sledge to his. It was never as far ahead as I had imagined. One couldn't see far in the pack, and normally a few minutes of us both pulling would suffice. I would feel so much happier when this happened. It was so demoralising to be left behind. Surely I couldn't have considered shooting him? But I had, and I'd worked out the logistics and rehearsed the consequences.

I didn't tell him about the incident until long after the journey was over. When I did confide it, Ran simply said he thought it was a perfectly reasonable and understandable response to the difficulties at the time.

Now I had no gun and there were no bears to carry away the body. I knew that these moods would go away if only I could keep going and crack the day. But why was I having them? In the Arctic they had disappeared after the first couple of weeks. As soon as I could keep up with Ran, I had stopped hating him and myself. I might not have been altogether happy, but the deep black shadows had receded from my mind. Here it was the opposite. For the first few weeks I had been all right, but now my moods were getting worse despite being ahead of Ran and the pulling easier for me. Why did I feel so bad?

If I couldn't shoot him, what could I do? I would have to be ill. Perhaps a sub-arachnoid haemorrhage – a burst blood vessel in the head which can occur spontaneously in young fit people. I could mimic it quite well. All I needed was a sudden pain in the back of the neck, and perhaps a bit of confusion to add reality to the seriousness. Ran wouldn't know what to make of it, and I could diagnose myself. I would simply tell him to call for urgent removal.

What if they came too quickly? If I was transported back to civilisation within a few days, it would entail my having a lumbar puncture – a large needle in the spine to check the diagnosis. I didn't fancy that much. I needed to think of another untreatable illness.

Appendicitis, kidney stones, back injuries, a complete alma-nac of possible medical conditions ranged through my head. Alternatively I could just decide to give up openly and frankly, to be proud of my human weakness rather than my inhuman dogged stupidity. After all, what sort of prat thought that it was macho to be on a crossing of Antarctica? The real challenges in life lay with people, relationships, spiritual development. You wouldn't catch D.H. Lawrence out here. No, I'll just call Ran and put it to him straight, and if he doesn't like it, he can stick it.

One or other plan was constantly close to fruition – I would be on the very verge of calling out 'Ran . . . Ran, stop! A pain . . . my neck.' It would be so easy, and after that there would be the tent and no restriction on food, then the aircraft, civilisation, and home. With luck, it would be only a week or so and I would be back with my family. I'd build that Wendy house immediately. I would be at peace, away from this awful, endless toil.

Would it be peace? Whatever I did to get out of the expedition I was going to have to live with for ever. I knew that within minutes of stopping I would want to go on again, for as soon as the load was relieved and the empty whiteness was replaced by the tent I would feel fine. Then I would be unable to go through with it and would just make a fool of myself in front of Ran. The thoughts echoed round and round my brain for every morning of every day – endless circles of repetitive consideration. I was steadily sinking into a deep deep pit, and always going nowhere.

Ran's mood, on the other hand, was improving almost daily since we had begun to eat more and his sledge became lighter. His problem must have been largely psychological – taking a few extra rations off a three hundred pound load couldn't make that much difference. He still found the pulling harder than I did, but, slow or not, he wouldn't be giving up or feigning illness. His determination was extraordinary, a drive quite beyond my understanding.

I turned to him for help and he tried to be encouraging and sympathetic. But really he failed to understand. I don't think he ever appreciated that I might actually give up, even before we had reached the Pole. Nevertheless, by telling him of my weakness and possible plans, I closed down all my avenues of escape. I warned him of the danger that I might feign illness and so deliberately made it almost impossible for myself. Then, on Day 54, I had a second bout of diarrhoea that was to cause the greatest difficulty in the journey so far. It was to alter our relationship profoundly and to precipitate a change in my trust and respect for Ran that would be very slow to recover.

We had set out as usual, but after a couple of hours I found myself repeatedly making stops, and with these urgent calls came stomach cramps and general weakness. Finally I told Ran that we would have to stop, but I didn't receive the anticipated sympathy. Instead he was angry.

'How long for?' he said testily, with a distinct edge to his voice.

'I don't know, Ran, but it's obvious that I can't go on like this.'

'All right, I don't mind, so long as when you're ready we finish the day and do the full number of hours.'

'Ran, I may not be ready. I don't know how long this will go on for.'

'Well, not now, but in a little while.' He deliberately mis-understood what I was saying. He didn't want to hear that I might not go on that day, but I wanted to make it quite clear.

'Look, this might be it for today. I don't know why I've got diarrhoea, but you just have to accept it.'

He wasn't pleased. We put up the tent in stilted silence. When we went inside, I noticed that he had only brought in the bare minimum of kit – he was making the point that he was not settling down for the day.

We made tea and I took Immodium tablets as I had on the previous occasion. Then I tried to settle down in my sleeping bag. In the next fifteen minutes I had to go out of the tent a couple of times, and each time I returned Ran asked if I was ready now. I ignored the questions and we became silent. Ran, seething about the enforced delay, concentrated on writing in his diary. I assumed he was making some sort of record of his anger with me.

My stomach began to settle, and as it did so, I could feel the sun shining through the fabric of the tent. It was warm on my face, and I could imagine lying on the lawn in the garden. Despite Ran, it was so good to have a rest, and we both needed it badly. I felt happy for the first time in many days and slowly drifted into sleep.

I woke after a couple of hours, feeling better and with the stomach cramps gone. I sat up with a view to making tea. I was not prepared for what Ran had to say.

'I've been working it out and I reckon that I could go on alone,' he announced. 'This is the second time we've had to stop for your diarrhoea, and we just have to be hard. If you can't take it, I am not going to wait for you.'

I listened in stunned silence. I was unable to believe what I was hearing. He hadn't finished.

'I have been feeling terrible for the last three weeks, and now, just as I get the bit between my teeth, you start holding things up. We're close to the Pole and we could easily arrange for you to be picked up by one of the aircraft going to the other expeditions. It wouldn't be very expensive.'

I started to feel the anger rising. From deep inside, it welled up to fill me with fury. I had been waiting for this man for the best part of two months as he did his stupid plod behind me. Now he had the bit between his teeth because I had part of his load on my sledge. How did he dare to threaten me for causing a brief delay?

'You bastard!' I almost hissed. 'There's no way that I am going to drop out now and let you go on alone, so don't even think it. It's you, not me, who can't take the pace. Now you'll just have to wait until I'm ready to go, like I've been waiting for you every day. This has nothing to do with my not being able to take it. It's to do with a short-lived stomach upset. In fact, I was feeling better and planning on our having tea and setting out again. Now I don't feel like doing anything of the sort.'

Ran suddenly looked shocked. I think he had surprised himself with what he had just done. Mind you, he couldn't claim it was a heat of the moment response. I could see that he had written out in his diary all the calculations to back up his theory. For a few moments neither of us said anything. Then he spoke again, softly now and with remorse.

'I'm sorry, I don't know what I was thinking of. It's just the frustration of having to stop when I had begun to feel better. I've felt so terrible for so long, and now, for the last few days, I've been feeling great again. Please believe it. I'm truly ashamed.'

He was too. It was there in his voice, and his eyes, but at that moment it made little difference to me. I had seen a side of him that I didn't like one bit. The nasty side which I had heard about so long ago before I had met him, but which he had buried while I was fit and strong. Perhaps it was the Devil that drove him. I doubted that I would ever trust him not to do the same again.

With an atmosphere that remained palpable, we made the tea and prepared to set off. We didn't speak, but as we finished drinking, he suddenly said, 'Mike, you're a real brick.' I was writing at the time and couldn't help but make the contrast – in my diary I wrote: 'Ran is a real prick.'

We set out again and made reasonable progress for a few hours but I had to make more emergency stops and towards the end of the afternoon was feeling pretty dreadful. Finally I became giddy and passed out. Suddenly I found myself lying on the snow, wondering what had happened. Ran came up and inquired, but he made no comment when I explained that the world had gone hazy and I had collapsed. Even then he didn't suggest stopping, although it must have been obvious that I was unable to continue. It shocked me once again. So much for his remorse. Determination was one thing, but this dementing pressure was quite another.

Although things superficially returned to normal in the days following this incident, I no longer trusted him. If that was his response to a straightforward acute problem, what would it be like when I began to weaken chronically, either physically or mentally. Looking beyond the Pole, I saw both of these as real possibilities. No, it seemed to me that my best policy was to guard against them. I had to maintain my mental and physical strength as best I could, even if it cost Ran his. I insisted that the sledges were corrected to even weights. Ran could fend for himself. If I pulled less now, I would be in a fitter state at the end, and anyway, I had no wish to help a man who would drop me just because things weren't going well. I also decided to go as fast as I liked and not to care if he became a dot. If it hurt Ran's morale, he could look after it himself, just as I had up in the Arctic.

This aggressive attitude helped me, and for a few days I had no problems with the black moods. I could get well ahead of Ran, and I felt no qualms when he came up and complained about my speed. He was probably hoping that I would take weight off him again but, as far as I was concerned, he could hope all the way to Scott Base. No, he was on his own for the rest of the trip and I would look after number one.

When not gloating over Ran's difficulties, I occupied my head with inanity. This consisted chiefly of silly songs, such as 'The Teddy Bear's Picnic' which I had sung to Tarn before leaving home. Others I made up as I went along, often sung to the tune of the 'Milky Bar Kid'. For some reason many were about our hens at home.

> The chickens they are big and strong,
> The chickens they can do no wrong
> They'll squawk and sing the whole night through
> They'll even squawk at me or you.

The chickens they can eat all day.
They'll even munch when they're at play.
They'll get so fat that they can't fly,
And then they'll squawk and probably die.

The chickens...

The song went on and on, sometimes for hours, pushing all else away. It was strange, but it made me happy and slowly, over many days, the anger began to fade. I began to come to terms with the fact that it must have been frustrating for Ran to have to stop. His reaction had been quite out of character, and such responses were part and parcel of these expeditions. One morning I gave a demonstration of my own capacity for graceless behaviour.

Ran's foot was much worse. Ever since the graft had broken down it had been getting worse and a deep ulcer was now eroding his forefoot. In the mornings it gave him hell, particularly when we had just started, and although he would generally steel himself and say nothing, occasionally even he would have to say something about the pain – try to share a part of it. Then he would be ashamed of himself, and call himself a wimp. I could do nothing but reassure him that I understood, though I didn't really. Pain is a problem that cannot be shared, certainly not with someone fighting his own battles.

Since the beginning of the expedition, we had been using 'skins' on the skis, a kind of synthetic fur strapped to the underside, with a nap which allowed them to slide forwards but not back. Our skis also had a 'fishscale' underside which could serve the same purpose, although not quite as effectively. One evening, with the sledges getting lighter, and a good surface, I tried pulling without the skins for the first time, and found some advantage. Although I tended to slip backwards more easily, there was much less resistance to sliding the ski forward and so, all in all, I worked less hard. The following morning, I tried it again, but temperatures had changed. The pulling was too difficult without them, and I kept slipping over backwards. I stopped and looked in my sledge, wanting to put the skins back on, but they were not there. I was horrified. I might be able to manage now, but we were sure to come across surfaces where pulling without them would be impossible.

'I've lost the skins,' I said to Ran.

He didn't seem to be interested. He was leaning on his sticks, grey with pain. I was too enmeshed with my own problem to see his.

'They've gone,' I repeated loudly. 'My skins aren't here. I must have left them on the snow when I took them off yesterday.'

He still didn't seem to register. He was looking down when he said, 'It's terrible. Every morning it's bloody terrible. I don't know how much more of it I can take.'

'Didn't you hear me? I've lost the skins. That's far more likely to stop the expedition than your bloody foot.'

Ran looked up startled, even puzzled, and then I realised what I'd done.

'I'm sorry,' I said humbly. 'That was as bad as you and the diarrhoea. I guess it's easy to make a prat of yourself out here.'

'Yes,' he replied thoughtfully. 'Yes, it is.'

The irony was that the skins were not even lost. I had put them into my night bag in order to check them over and found them there that evening in the tent. However, the incident had been useful – Ran could now cite it whenever the diarrhoea episode was mentioned. It was tit for tat.

Day 60 passed. The Pole was now close, perhaps only a week away, or less if the surfaces improved, but instead of my morale lifting it began to fall again. I really didn't know if I could go on beyond for another nine hundred empty miles. It seemed such an obvious place to give up, and we had heard that that was exactly what the American women were going to do. They had originally planned to do as we were, to cross the continent and reach the same ship at Scott Base, but now they were only a few miles ahead of us, despite starting more than one hundred and fifty miles in front on the edge of the land, rather than on the ice-shelf. They had also been resupplied from the air en route, and so had relatively light sledges. If they were to go on from the Pole, budget limitations would force them to make the second half of their journey unsupported, and then their sledges would be much heavier. Having set out ten days late, as we did, and encountering the same disappointing surfaces on the plateau, they now recognised that they were moving far too slowly. They had decided that to go on was not possible and that they would be flying home from the Pole.

To join them seemed so tempting. Yet at the same time I wanted to go on. In particular, I wanted to reach the Trans-Antarctic mountains and to see the Beardmore Glacier. We had spent so long in this blank white empty wilderness and now I wanted the reward. From earlier expeditions, I knew how spectacular Antarctica could be. That grandeur was ours if we could only make it across the remainder of the plateau. I needed to go on, yet a part of me was once again looking for excuses. Feeling happier with Ran, I reiterated my warning of my own potential weakness. This time my message seemed to hit home. It was as if he suddenly realised that I was serious and that I might go ahead and drop out. He saw that, if we were to be successful, he needed to help me if he could, and he suddenly began to talk of his own source of strength in a way that I had never heard before.

'I don't know if it can help you,' he said one night as we had just settled down to sleep, 'but I get my strength from God. Every night, just at this moment, I pray and ask for his help.'

He was speaking in earnest, and he sat up and looked over at me. I knew already that he was a religious man, but until then I hadn't realised the depth of his belief. Not being religious myself, it didn't really help me.

'I also do it for my family,' he continued. 'Not just Ginny, but the whole clan that's in here' – he indicated his chest. 'They're all there, my father, my grandparents, all of them rooting for me, and giving me strength. You should see your family inside you, and realise that you are doing this for them.'

I didn't know what to say. I felt embarrassed by his honesty. As far as my wife was concerned, she would probably prefer that I gave up and came home. Although to some extent she understood why I did it, she also thought of this sort of venture as being fairly pointless. At that moment I wasn't sure that I didn't agree with her. But my overall motivation was not the issue. It was the day to day difficulty of keeping going when the going was so hard that it took one so close to the edge.

'And then there's Britain,' Ran said. 'I want to see someone British succeed in doing this, and if we don't, it will be men from Norway, or Germany, or Japan who do it. It's about time that England had something to be proud of.'

This was of no value to me either. I am no ardent patriot. I believe that the differences between nations are of value but not as a matter of superiority. No, I would have to rely on my reluctance to lose face to keep me going on a day to day basis. Perhaps in the longer term my desire to see those mountains would be enough. I no longer thought that we could reach Scott Base, but perhaps we could descend the Beardmore and get out on to the ice-shelf. We could still complete the first unsupported crossing of the continent.

Two days from the Pole, questions of motivation and going on came very close to being superfluous. It was a windy day, but the sun was shining when I came out of the tent and it seemed relatively warm. I set off with just my lightweight cotton sledge-jacket, worn over long underwear and my fleece salopettes. I chose only thin contact gloves to wear inside my outer mitts.

After an hour or so, the wind had risen and I became very cold. In particular, my hands were suffering badly and not warming up. Ran was still following because he had had problems with icing on his goggles and glasses in the freezing wind and had asked me to continue leading for as long as I didn't mind. He was therefore there to help when my hands became so bad that I had to get some extra mittens out of my sledge and found that my fingers were unable to pull them on. The pain was unbearable, and despite myself, I was whimpering like an injured dog when Ran came up. He tried to help, tugging at the cuffs, but still they wouldn't go on. Seeing how desperate I was, Ran took off his own warm mitts and gave them to me. He then struggled into my cold ones, which were far too small for him. It was a wonderful gesture.

I set off again, badly chilled after the long stop and barely able to pull the sledge. I was getting into real trouble. After failing to get any warmer by going faster, I realised that I had to stop and put on my fleece jacket. To do this meant removing the sledge-jacket completely, and once again I had trouble with my fingers. This time I was unable to do up the zips on the jackets. After struggling for a couple of minutes I couldn't even get Ran's larger mitts back on. I had entered the vicious circle again. By the time I was dressed again, my thinking was beginning to fade. I kept walking for another half-hour but was never warm and not fully conscious. It is only through Ran's later description that I know what then took place.

He said that I had been walking along very slowly when I began to wander from side to side. As I had been in front for more than two hours and his glasses were somewhat better, he had come up and suggested taking over the lead. I had passed the compass when he asked for it, but he sensed that something was wrong, despite being unable to see my covered face. He asked if I was all right and received an unintelligible garbled noise in reply. Immediately he thought that I must be hypothermic.

'I tried to get you to help me put up the tent,' he told me, 'but you were just standing around doing nothing, so I put it up by myself and pushed you inside. I wanted you to light the stove but you just knelt there in the middle, completely still and unresponsive. You were in the same position when I came back a couple of minutes later after I had unpacked your sledge and thrown your sleeping bag inside. I shouted at you again to light the stove, and opened the box and gave you the matches. Then I went to get my things from the other sledge. I was another couple of minutes and, when I returned, you had started to light the stove and seemed a little more with it. Perhaps you were better for being out of the wind. Mind you, you weren't exactly compos mentis, and I had to get you into your sleeping bag and make you drink some tea. It was about half an hour before you started making real sense and to appreciate what had happened.'

His diagnosis was correct of course. I probably had been hypothermic although my recovery was faster than might be expected. I wondered whether it was actually a combination of hypothermia and hypoglycaemia – a low blood sugar. After all, we had been exercising hard and not eating adequately, and the symptoms of the two conditions are almost indiscernible. Furthermore, they can occur together. If you get low on blood sugar, it prevents you from either shivering properly or being able to constrict the blood vessels in your skin to limit heat loss.

Whatever the diagnosis, I realised that I had been incredibly lucky. On most days Ran and I made changes of the compass without a word, and indeed if it hadn't been for Ran's glasses misting, he might well have been out in front when I started running into trouble. I would then have been struggling with my gloves and jacket alone, and probably without success. I could easily have become more deeply hypothermic. I would then have wandered about until I collapsed, and my survival time would have been negligible. By the time Ran had realised that I wasn't behind him, tracks would have been blown to oblivion and he would never have found me.

Ran also realised that we had been fortunate and, after I had recovered, wanted to discuss our position. He was very concerned by this new vulnerability.

'Mike, if you become hypothermic with all your clothes on and moving,' he said gravely, 'what will it be like when we've lost even more weight and the conditions are worse on the far side of the Pole? The journey could easily end in tragedy, and giving up at the Pole would be no shame. I think we should seriously consider pulling out before it's too late.'

I thought about it and could see the truth in what he said. The season was advancing, and we would be going even higher beyond the Pole. At the same time, the whole of the day's events had been triggered by my dressing incorrectly in the first place. I had simply misjudged how cold it was when I set off inadequately dressed.

'I don't want to stop, and I think we can ascribe today's particular problem to my own stupidity and it being particularly cold. If, from now on, I follow the policy of starting off with all my clothing on, and then removing it if I get too hot, I would have thought it would be safe.'

'Well, I suppose you're right,' he agreed, 'though today didn't seem all that cold until we made all those stops. We're both going to have to turn round much more often and make certain at every changeover that the other party is all right.'

EIGHT

★

A Step Through Time

ON DAY 68 we came in sight of the dome of the American Station at the South Pole. I felt the tears flooding my eyes as I approached. For so many years I had wanted to achieve just this. I had watched the Footsteps of Scott team depart on their walk to the Pole. I had been desperate to join them, believing that I would never have another chance to go on a Polar expedition. After that Ran and I had repeatedly failed to reach the North Pole, and it had seemed that I was destined never to reach either end of the earth. Now I was here, and had arrived in a way unequalled before. It did not look a grand or romantic place, rather a depressing eyesore created by the research station. Even their marking of the exact site of the Pole – a striped barber's sign topped by an enlarged silver Christmas bauble – was tacky. Nevertheless nothing could spoil this moment for me.

We arrived walking side by side to avoid precedence and saw the American women's expedition waiting to welcome us. They had arrived twenty-four hours earlier, having demonstrated that women could perfectly well take on the worst environment that nature could offer. It was good to see them, and after some photographs and film were taken, we set up our tent and invited them inside.

It was strange to be with other company after more than two months alone. For about an hour, we had a wonderful conversation. They may not have pulled the same weights as we had, but they had been through exactly the same hardships over an almost identical period. We knew that they would be some of the very, very few people who would ever fully understand what it had been like for us, and we shared this understanding with mutual pleasure.

While we were talking, we learned more of Ehrling Kagge who had succeeded in reaching the Pole more than a week before. We had already known of his success from Mo, a very fast journey which alone must have been so difficult. On first hearing of it, I had been filled with admiration. When I learned that it had been announced to the world as another Norwegian triumph over the British, I had believed that Kagge himself had not claimed a win. He had made it quite clear to me back in Punta that he appreciated that our journeys were so different. It had to be the sensationalist press that had created the story for their own ends. I was mistaken. We learned from the American women that, when Kagge had flown out to Patriot Hills, he personally had stated that he viewed it as a race which he had won. We were told he even went so far as to say that when he had met us in South America Mike Stroud had seen it in the same light. I was truly disappointed. Although I had never agreed with Kagge's interpretation of unsupported as it had applied in the North, I had always believed him to be honest. Now I thought he was mean-spirited. It is a pity that the world's media were not more discriminating.

All the same, we were only halfway through our journey and we could do nothing better to refute Kagge's claim than to carry on. Then people would see for themselves that our undertaking was in a different league. Every step we took from now on would hurt him.

The time flew by. Talking to other people was so refreshing, but it was time to go. We had limited ourselves to an hour at the Pole. I had a letter for Thea, which I had written over the previous few days, and gave it to one of the women who would pass it to Mo and it would be flown out.

> . . . *Ran believes in an Ethiopia style trek, but I am not sure we can do it. I must admit that my greatest fear is that I would want to give up before him. In fact I already have wanted to, but managed to resist. But don't worry, I will give up if necessary and with luck we will have some wind and will be able to leave half rations to a more realistic last couple of weeks. Don't take this as*

over confidence, but I actually believe that the most likely outcome will be a failure of the trip on the Ross ice-shelf. That would be a shame, but much better than we could have expected and we would still have crossed the continent, done all the science, and hopefully the MS fund raising would have gone well . . . It can't be too long now since we don't have much food. I'll be home thin but happy within a few weeks. Meanwhile hug the children for me and give Callan the little note which I hope he can read himself, and Tarn the drawing (I always knew I should have been an artist!) Pass my news to the family, and forward the little notes to my mother and father.   *All my love, Mike*

As well as sending out our messages, we also received some notes from Mo, among them congratulations from many of our sponsors. There was also some bad news. Adventure Network was now insisting that Mo would have to leave the Antarctic on the 24/25th January when they would be cutting their operation right back in preparation for the coming winter. It was only a few days away, and we would still be high on the plateau and very vulnerable. An ANI staff member from Chile, Alejo, would take over our communications and Mo was busy teaching him everything he might need to know. She would stay in South America, in contact with him, and so be able to interpret our brief messages and hence gain a true understanding of what was going on as we pushed towards our distant goal. But we were going to miss her voice terribly in our tent. It was a voice that we had grown to love and which lifted our spirits nightly.

Just before we took down the tent and left the Pole we stripped to our underwear and popped outside. The Christmas bauble was surrounded by an equally tasteful piece of plywood, quite why I cannot imagine. But it served our purpose well as we weighed ourselves again, probably the best quality data we had gathered so far. It was not encouraging. I had now shed forty pounds and Ran's losses were approaching fifty. These were huge losses, well above my wildest estimates before departure. If I had been asked, I would have said that they were incompatible with towing sledges as we had done. It was not surprising that we had not been getting faster.

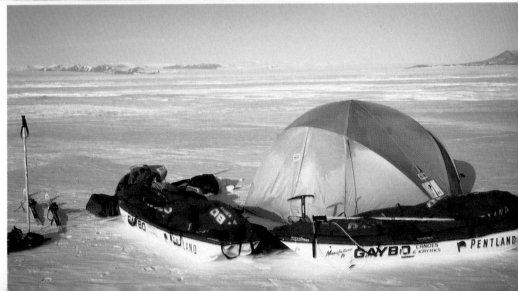

19 Entering the glacier system

20 Mike negotiating the blue-ice with a damaged ankle

21 Ran fashioning his
   paracord 'crampons'

22 Mike dressing a
   frostbitten finger

23 Ran with no sticks on blue-ice

24 Mike seeking a crevasse
   crossing

25 Camping beyond the
   Wedge Face crevasses

When we left we deliberately avoided the buildings of the Pole station. In that way we could claim that we had received no support of any kind, even at the level of simple hospitality. If we couldn't avoid man's desecration, we could still attempt to keep our journey as pure as it could be. Yet, despite our efforts, it was reported in Britain that 'When the explorers reached the Pole, they went inside for tea and were checked over by a doctor.' The mythical doctor was even quoted in the papers, describing us as 'thin but fit'. It was another sad example of press inaccuracy.

Moving away, I wept. It was so hard to wave goodbye to the American women who suddenly seemed like our closest friends, and who later that afternoon would fly out and be on their way home. We faced more hunger, cold and pain, and probably all for nothing. There were nearly nine hundred miles of ice ahead of us, and most of it would continue to provide an empty horizon, despite now heading north.

The Pole changed nothing. On the following day we were back in the same old routine, the endless circle that we had been repeating for so long. It was as if we had never been there, never had a break. The days just went on like a recurring nightmare.

We were weakening fast. It was not far beyond the Pole that we recognised our malnourishment. On a day of deep, deep cold, and as the end of the fifth long hour approached, I began feeling utterly fatigued, not the same old tiredness that we had been feeling throughout the expedition but a new sensation, as if running on empty. From our weights at the Pole, we knew that we were eating nowhere near enough and were becoming debilitated. What we needed was a boost before we faded altogether. We would perish without extra food to get us off the plateau and on to the top of the glaciers. After that we could cut right back and try to survive on half rations as we went downhill. With luck, we would even have following winds and – who knows? – we might still be able to make Scott Base. If not, and we only managed to reach the ice-shelf, we would still be the first to cross the continent without aircraft.

It would still be the longest unsupported journey ever made. We just had to be realistic.

At the end of the hour I watched Ran catch me up. I could see that he too was completely done in. There was an air of dejection about him. He knew we were facing defeat.

'We're both stuffed, Ran, and we know it,' I said. 'Why don't we miss the next hour, and stop to have some soup now? We could then do a couple of hours before talking this evening.'

He didn't answer immediately but started to take off his harness. Then, as he moved wearily back to his sledge, he spoke.

'I guess you're thinking about increasing the food, drawing in our horns and limiting ourselves to the bottom of the Beardmore.'

I was astonished. First, that he was ready to give up even one hour of the day, something which normally he would have dismissed as weak-minded, and second, because he was thinking along exactly the same lines. Clearly we were feeling just as bad as one another. That evening, sitting with our mugs of tea, we made new plans.

'I think that we should eat one extra ration over the next couple of days,' I started, 'and then say three more over the following twelve. With a bit of wind, that should take us beyond the edge of the plateau, and we can decide when we get to the glaciers how we go on from there. It will depend on how we feel, and how far we've got.'

'I agree,' Ran said, 'but only if we can save the chocolate, flapjacks and soups as before. I also reckon that, whatever happens, we should still switch to half rations on Day 84 so that we're covered until Day 109. Although we'd have to stop a couple of days before that if we aren't going to make it to Scott Base. An aircraft could take days to reach us.'

'Well, I'm happy with saving the goodies, but I'm not so sure about the half rations. We can try it, but I'll bet it will be absolute hell. Frankly, we are already starving, and God knows what it will be like on less. I just can't imagine it.'

'We'll manage,' he said. 'If we can just go as fast as Messner did, Scott Base might still be in range.'

'That may be true,' I cautioned, 'but Messner would have been far stronger than we are. He started two hundred miles closer in, pulled light sledges, was resupplied en route, and rested at the South Pole. He also got a fair bit of wind after the Pole, didn't he?'

Ran opened the notes in his diary. 'Yes. Yes, he did. In fact after the Pole, while on the plateau, he hardly manhauled at all. When the wind wasn't blowing, they simply stopped and waited for it.'

'If only...' I murmured, 'but it must come sometime.'

Each day began according to the watch. The tent filtered light from twenty-four hour sunshine, giving no clues as to the time. Around seven in the morning GMT, Ran would crawl out of his bag and put on the coffee. Then he would busy himself for about ten minutes, making all sorts of arrangements that I never quite understood. If I stirred during this period, he seemed to find it disturbing. It was a part of the day that was his own and he sought the privacy to follow his routine. He was a methodical man who liked his days well organised.

Around 7.20 the coffee would be ready. The dry Antarctic air dehydrated us overnight and we awoke with throats parched and enjoyed the drink. Then I took over the stove to cook our breakfast. I had done the cooking on all of our journeys together. Ran never enjoyed it, and I was quite happy with the arrangement. It took about twenty minutes to prepare, fifteen for the ice to melt and boil, and then five to let the freeze-dried porridge stand. That was the frustrating part. Our stomachs craved to be filled, yet we had learned that the craving would be that bit more satisfied if we were patient. We had only realised it at the end of the last Arctic trip. Before that we had simply added the boiling water and butter, stirred it up and wolfed it down. Then, after calling for the helicopter on the very last day, I had made the porridge and for the first time was in less of a hurry to eat it. While talking, we had let it stand for a few minutes, and before our eyes it had swelled, doubling or more in volume. Slowly it dawned on us that for four years of travel together we had been stupid. With a little

121

more patience, we could have had what would have felt like far larger breakfasts. Now we waited, mouths watering in expectation, for the onset of heaven. The bland hot cereal was ambrosia from the gods.

By about 8.15 we were dressing to go outside, a slow process since it required the utmost care. When putting on socks and boots, it was so easy to get your socks rucked, especially while wearing three pairs. Once walking, one tended not to stop for adjusting footwear which was just too much trouble. Instead I would press on, even if a hot spot was bothering me and a blister resulted. No, care had to come at the outset. One little fold could destroy one's feet for the rest of the trip. Around half past eight Ran would go out of the tent and start taking off the fly sheet and dismantling the radio antenna. Inside, after relishing that short moment of relaxation, I would take a small brush and sweep the thick rime ice from the roof and walls. It took about five minutes, and then I too went out into the cold.

Ran would be hobbling. His damaged foot hurt most when he first started walking on it. He must have been fighting a constant urge to call it a day. It was painful to watch him for you could see the effort of will that it took. He soon looked pale and drained. Generally he didn't say much but he didn't have to – the raw nerves, grinding against his boot, painted their message across his taut features. Occasionally he had to vocalise it, cursing his foot with pent-up bitterness. Then he would apologise.

'I'm sorry. You don't want to hear all this. I feel such a bloody wimp.'

'Don't even say it, Ran. I'm just sorry I can't help. I would have been far worse than you.'

It was true. I think few men could have faced the prospect of hundreds of miles of walking with infection and frost eating into their feet. Most would have given up long ago, probably with me among them, grateful for the excuse. Sometimes I wondered about women. Would they be able to tolerate these things better than we did?

It was an interesting question. After returning from Siberia, I had written a layman's report of my scientific findings for a

Saturday newspaper feature. The following week there was a letter from a female nutritionist which said that, although my findings were interesting, I had not mentioned that perhaps females would be better suited for such expeditions: first, because they carried more fat than men and so would have a good fuel supply; and second, they were more resilient and could tolerate pain and discomfort better. There was probably a lot of truth in what she had said, but the last paragraph had sounded a different note. The writer suggested that since these expeditions were prime examples of the heroically daft, where men might see the heroism, all women would see was the daftness.

Many of the days were bright and sunny and I would start off leading, heading for the north, guided by my shadow. In order to use our shadows for navigation, and to prevent the low sun from shining directly in our eyes, we always moved with the sun behind us. Before the Pole, this had meant walking during the local geographic daytime, with the sun in the east as we started, on our backs to the north in the middle of our day and to the west, on our right, when we stopped. This had allowed us to head southwards, using our watches, avoiding the need for endless consultations of the compass which was slow to settle so close to the magnetic Pole. Now that we had passed the geographic Pole, all this had changed. Local daytime would have seen us walking into the sun since, in a single stride as we passed the Pole, and without a change in direction, we had moved from walking south in the western hemisphere to walking north in the eastern. We had effectively switched from day to night, and perhaps even more strangely, changed from one date to the next. The result was that our morning start now corresponded to local evening, and when we set off, I walked with the sun to the west.

At first the bitter cold and the sunshine would stimulate me, and I would hurry forward, seeking warmth from exertion and feeling quite happy with life. Then, after only a few minutes, the fatigue would come and my legs would start their constant cry for respite. Soon the huge task ahead of us seemed more impossible than ever, and my mind quickly became sick with the constant effort. With the Pole not far back, it was more tempting than ever to give up. Comfort, safety and food could be had so easily, and these three Sirens were so hard to ignore. It was too far to go, and soon dark clouds that had already gathered at the horizon of my consciousness pushed forward to blot out the sunshine. I was back to fighting with my feigned illness and excuses. Sometimes these clouds had even gathered before I left the tent, and I had to blow them away with an effort of will. On the march, I knew that I couldn't prevent their intrusion, but in the tent I would tenaciously defend my hours of sanity. They were too few to be lost to the black oppression.

We continued to alternate the lead every hour, but by this stage the first six periods had become stretched to an hour and a half or more, with only the last couple close to the normal length. I knew that if I could continue for the first half of the day, the mental pressures would ease, but the hands of my watch would stand still and the day passed interminably slowly.

At about two o'clock we had our first break, pulling the broken thermos out of Ran's sleeping bag. Unpleasant coagulated globs of suet in the lukewarm soup cloyed the mouth and stuck in the throat. They were followed by a couple of squares of chocolate, more food from the heavens. It was too cold for proper rest and five minutes was about the maximum. At the Pole we had learned that for the last few weeks temperatures on the plateau had rarely exceeded minus 40°C, and with windchill it had effectively been much colder. Indeed, on the day that I had become hypothermic, the Pole – only a few miles away – had had a windchill of minus 83°C. It was little wonder that I had run into trouble.

After the stop, we hauled on for a further four and a half hours, and as my shadow crossed before me, the clouds in my mind parted. Once the day was broken, I usually received the strength to see it through to the end. It was all a question of a bit less shame. With half the day completed, one might as well finish it and go a few extra miles. It wasn't that I suddenly felt happy, more that I would now plod on intending to call it all off that evening. With that decided, my thoughts became wider, although they still didn't return to those constructive thoughts of the early part of the trip. Instead, they were locked in Antarctica. It was really only during the first thirty or forty days that I had been able to escape into day-dreams. For the last thirty, if I wasn't thinking of giving up or singing about chickens, I had generally thought of logistics. How long could we make the food last? How weak would we get? Would we get some help from wind?

Only towards the end of our day, when the sun lay to the east, did I rid my mind of these circular and unanswerable questions. Only then could I look around with unclouded eyes and see the beauty of where we walked – its glorious solitude and the endless variety of textured surfaces.

Although past the Pole, we had yet to reach the maximum height of our journey. We continued to cross undulating but slowly rising ground, the ups and downs just as crushing as previously. The only change was that the surfaces had become somewhat firmer. Often we found them blown into a thin crust which caused a strange phenomenon that I had noticed on earlier visits to Antarctica. While you were walking along, the surface would settle abruptly, not just under your feet but extending away from you with a loud elongated crunch. It obviously happened where surface crust covered a hollow, and generally it was a brief, one-off event in a small area. Here the same thing was happening everywhere. We would drop suddenly about six inches, always getting a bit of a shock that made you think you were going into a crevasse. Then, instead of the noise just spreading a little way from you, the triggered settling would travel for hundreds of yards. Sometimes it would go in a full circle, and you would suddenly hear the sound coming back to you from a different direction. It was like a jet aircraft approaching. Acres of ice were dropping just a few inches, echoing the first passing of human footsteps.

Was it the first passing? Before the Pole we had walked over land that had never before been trod, but now we were following the route taken by Captain Scott and his party, and more recently by Robert Swan and my other Footsteps companions. Messner must also have travelled near here. None may have passed at exactly this location, but they too had

followed their shadows across these bleak wastes, leaving no
sign of their passing.

> . . . I will show you something different from either
> Your shadow at morning striding behind you
> Or your shadow at evening rising to meet you;
> I will show you fear in a handful of dust.

T.S. Eliot's words from *The Waste Land* rang in my mind as I
looked about with the eyes of those who had gone before us.

How had it been for Scott and his men when they headed
for the coast eighty years before? By that time, they had been
to the Pole and had seen Amundsen's small tent. In it, they had
found the letter which told them that they had been beaten to
their goal by over a month. They must have been decimated.
Even though the expedition had a comprehensive scientific
programme, precedence to the Pole underlay their motivation.
Why was that? Is there a compulsion in the human psyche to
achieve or witness such 'firsts'? Certainly, being the first was
important for me, although I was unsure whether this was
because it increased the challenge, and hence led to greater
satisfaction, or because it led to the promise of louder public
acclaim at the end. Whatever my motivation, it is only a lucky
few who can make a brief note on the pages of history and
I sometimes wondered what substitute the true adventurer
would find in future when no first journey is left to be made
on earth. Of course there are other planets, and for some there
is always the contrived, although I for one would never leave
my armchair for athletic records such as the Antarctic by pogo
stick in under eighty days. I can see it now – league tables
of the fastest unsupported crossings by teams from nation
states, no doubt in an ever diminishing Olympic record time
and with a few tragic disasters, our chasing for a more fundamental target in 1993 remembered as the first and slowest of
many long forgotten record-breakers to follow. The appeal for
us had much more to do with attempting something which the
right-minded deemed to be impossible.

How did we compare with Scott? In which ways did our
journey differ significantly from theirs?

Beaten to their goal and heading back north, Scott and

his men would no doubt have been more tired, hungry and depressed than were we. Their journey to the Pole had been slower than ours, and although each had been pulling less weight, they had been eating even more inadequately. Recently much has been made of their vitamin deficiencies when explaining their declining health and ultimately their death. However, Ran and I had burned 8,000 calories a day to reach the Pole. Admittedly the weights we pulled were greater than Scott's, and we had had no lay-up days since that storm nearly two months before, but I reckon that Scott and his men would have been working as strenuously as we were, struggling as hard as they could for as long as they could each day. If that were so, then they must have had an average expenditure of at least 6,000 calories, and since their daily rations contained almost a thousand calories less than our own, their starvation must have been worse than ours. By the time they reached the Pole, they had probably lost more weight than we had, and returning, things could only have been getting worse. They probably would have died even if they had not been vitamin deficient. Hauling sledges from the coast of Antarctica to the Pole has a savage effect on the body.

What of their psychology? As they struggled through their day – experiencing the same settling surfaces, the same cold, and the same tired legs – what did they think of? Ahead lay a line of depots stretching back to their base on the far side of the ice-shelf. They aimed to pick them up one by one, so their sledge would be relatively light all the way back to their cosy hut. They must have dreamt continually of that hut; it had been their home for the previous year and all their companions were there. I had visited it many times when on the Footsteps expedition. We had lived two hundred yards along the beach from it. The seventy-five years hadn't touched it. It was literally frozen in time and you could feel the occupancy. Yet it also had the air of utmost desolation, an emptiness that only the Antarctic could generate. The hut stood waiting for those who never were to come.

When did they realise the threat that hung over them? Did they believe at this stage that they could do it? With their hunger must have come malaise, and they were aware that they would be returning to acknowledge defeat rather than to bask in victory. They had frostbite, and seaman Evans had damaged his hand when repairing a sledge on the way to the Pole. It was festering. He had kept this a secret, in case he had not been allowed to go on, but now the others knew of it and saw that he couldn't keep up. They must have known that it threatened all their lives, but when did they come to terms with their probable end? It must have been dawning as they crossed this same empty landscape.

Following the announcement that we had successfully man-hauled to the Pole, several newspaper articles in Britain belittled our efforts, saying that in the modern age, with better equipment and communications, it was all too easy. This was a simplistic view. As far as the pulling was concerned, I doubt that things were very different. Our sledges were constructed of better materials than Scott's but our loads were much greater. Scott's men were eating relatively less, and were probably weaker, but we weren't exactly replete and there must be a limit to how hungry one can feel. Strangely, we were probably colder. Although modern clothing is better in some ways, synthetic fabrics have no magic, and our extreme lightweight approach had limited our clothing so radically that we wore far less than they had done. A tent is also a tent, and our little dome, although much lighter than Scott's pyramid, was no warmer. At this high altitude, it was no longer the sun-warmed shelter that we had experienced earlier, and we had lost much of our bodies' insulation. Like Scott and his men, we were now cold for much of the day and at night. Camping trips in the Polar regions could never be holidays. All in all, there seemed to be more similarities than differences.

There was, of course, one great contrast. Whatever the threats to our health and comfort, we knew that we were unlikely to die. We had communications, and if things didn't work out, we could call for help. We could also receive messages from our families that were a tremendous psychological boost. Mind you, communications was not the guarantee of safety that the newspapers made out. They painted a picture in which, if we got into trouble, we simply pressed the red button and an aircraft arrived – ill or injured, we would be out in no time.

This was laughable. By now Adventure Network aircraft were more than a thousand miles away. They were too small to fly to us without refuelling, and to reach us they would have to go via depots. Each take-off and landing could be made only in good weather, and as the season progressed, the chances of an aircraft being able to fly on any given day were rapidly diminishing. By the end of our journey, it would be a matter of luck if they were able to fly on one day in any five.

Furthermore, even to have them come, we would have to get through to Mo on the radio. We were in an area of the world that was well known for poor radio reception. Even Mo's skill and diligence could not guarantee that we could be heard. Just one major auroral storm and the ionosphere would be destroyed for days. With radio contact lost we would not be in the position described by those papers. It was not a question of picking up a phone and asking for a taxi to the station.

Indeed, you could argue that having communications put a psychological stress on us that was not experienced by Scott. If I wanted to – and I have said that I often did – I could call for evacuation and stop the expedition. This was the pressure that I found the greatest. It was the source of all those dark clouds. Beyond all physical pain and tiredness, beyond the hunger and fears, it was the pressure that lay at the heart of my difficulties. I had lived with it almost daily for the past six weeks and I could dearly have done without it. I would even have considered increasing the risks to escape the torture of that dilemma.

We had our second soup soon after six in the evening from the flask that was working, hot and much more pleasant. Then we set off again, generally in better spirits. It was now only two hours until the sun would lie to the east and once more our shadows would be at right angles to our course. The anticipation of the tent made these hours pleasurable. Another day broken, that was the attitude. One less day to go.

Once we had stopped, we erected the tent and Ran would hurriedly throw his things inside and rush in. This was another moment of privacy that he treasured, the chance to sort himself out according to a repeated daily ritual. I would stay outside for longer. Although Ran put up the radio antenna, I had the other evening jobs to do – guying out the tent in case a storm blew up; collecting snow or ice blocks by the door, and finally attending to my broken sledge. It was still holding together, despite the odds, but it filled with snow and needed digging out every day. I also needed to tighten the runner screws and my makeshift straps. It took only five minutes but it was a pain. At the end of eleven or twelve hours of hauling all one wanted to do was to get inside that tent and light the stove.

While I was outside, Ran would also organise my kit so that when I came in it was tidy and welcoming. He would then put on the tea while I removed my iced clothing. All gloves, hats and goggles were hung in the roof to dry, and frost was brushed off the inside of jackets before they were folded up in the corner. Boots were also carefully brushed to remove frost from the shell, inners and gaiters. Then I would unpack my diary, a ration and some other bits and pieces. Lastly I would take out the satellite navigator which we were using to check our position. I would hang this in the top of the tent roof to thaw out, and once the batteries and electronics were warm, we could learn of the day's progress. At least, we could if it were working. The device relied upon estimating its own position from the positions of several satellites, receiving signals from them and cross-checking the information. Because we were still so close to the Pole, longitude information was especially vulnerable to error. After all, at the Pole itself, one position corresponded to all possible longitudes. The machine wasn't built to be intelligent. It could not understand why it was being told slightly different values and frequently decided that it could give us only the simple message ... ERROR.

When the ice had melted and the water boiled, I would make two brimming cups of tea. We drank them with a flapjack which had been thawed and warmed on the top of the pot. We also ate a few squares of chocolate if we had managed to resist consuming them all during the day. Chocolate tasted so much better if it wasn't frozen and could be sucked, savoured, and made to last. During the day, this was almost impossible, and the pieces would be gone in moments. One of life's few pleasures would have been stolen. The early evening was the best part of the day – hauling was over and relaxation had begun. I used to forget my resolution to abandon the journey, and think that, with luck and determination, it was still possible. That short-term memory was acting again.

Every tenth day, there was an unwelcome variation in our routine when I conducted the blood tests for our science programme. I always wanted to take the samples before we had eaten or drunk anything, in order that they reflected the state of our blood sugar, fats and hormones at the end of a period of work. On those days I would come into the tent and immediately produce syringes and needles. This would horrify Ran, and grimacing, he would lie down, face to the tent wall, and refuse to look at what was going on. Unfortunately he then had to take a sample from me, and since he also refused to look then, I was not filled with confidence.

Once taken, the blood samples were transferred into tubes with anti-coagulant, and hung high up to keep warm until shortly before we went to sleep. During that time the red blood cells would settle to the bottom of the tubes, leaving a small volume of clear plasma above. At the end of the evening I used a little pipette to take this plasma off, and then put it in small containers and left it to freeze. The samples were to be taken back to England for analysis, and would tell us, after it was all over, something of how our bodies were coping with the horrendous stresses.

As well as blood samples, I also took small samples of urine every day, and on five occasions during the trip, we both made twenty-four hour urine studies. These latter tests were the most unwelcome part of our programme – barring those needle muscle biopsies which we remembered with horror and looked forward to with dread. For a whole day and night, instead of peeing in the snow, one of us would use the pee bottle to make a cumulative collection. Using a narrow-neck bottle outside in the wind, was quite different from using it in the tent. It inevitably led to a good deal of discomfort for both the hands and other parts. Twice I even got a touch of penile frostbite.

After tea the stove would be left running to melt ice for water for the next day's flasks. While this was taking place, Ran and I would write in our diaries and talk about our progress. It was normally at this stage that the Magellan, if working, was warm enough to tell us how far we had travelled. The result was invariably disappointing and would lead to our speculating about our chances. Ran was still following a pessimistic line in order to avoid giving himself false hopes. He would announce that, even doing ten miles a day, we could reach Mount Ward and the top of the glaciers in 'x' days. The 'x' was always too high. For me, the tent and the rest always brought optimism and I had to see things improving. If x was really to be that long, I felt it would kill me. I believed that we would get some wind from behind, as Messner had. Then we could reach the mountain within days rather than weeks.

Our relationship was now good again. Even if we differed in outlook, the achievement of the Pole and our continuing progress had healed the rifts. I had more or less forgiven Ran for the nasty episode with the diarrhoea. It was just an act out of character, triggered by the stress and frustration at the time. He was still slower and it now seemed reasonable to start lightening his sledge once more. We agreed to start taking two days' fuel and food off his sledge for every one from mine. Nevertheless I was still concerned that this would see me reaching my physical limits before he did. Although he stated firmly now that he would not go on without me, I was not entirely confident in him and was always ready to start handing back the weight if necessary.

Once the soups were made, I would start cooking the main meal, although cooking is perhaps a rather grand euphemism for adding hot water to a freeze dried mush. Mind you, there was the exciting culinary flexibility of putting in a little more or a little less butter, and despite the simplicity of food production, what we finally ate would be delicious. At ten o'clock we made radio contact with Mo. This was often no more than a brief exchange of 'all okay's. We said as little as possible in order to conserve our radio batteries – a radio uses ten times as much power on transmit as it does on receive. However, we could listen without using too much battery life while Mo provided us with messages from home, or other information from our patron, sponsors, or the MS Society.

Of course she would be leaving soon, despite a short reprieve from the date we had been given at the Pole. Now she was to go out on our Day 80. We would miss her. Her voice in our little tent had become an important part of our day, and when she relayed news from our wives, we knew that earlier she, a friend, had been talking to them. It gave the messages a personal quality that somebody else just couldn't match. So often Mo's sharp wit coming over the airwaves had brightened our moods and broken the tension between us. We always enjoyed hearing of the practical jokes she had played at the Patriot Hills camp.

When Mo and her husband Flo had first joined us in the Arctic for the second of our North Pole attempts, we were forced to wait for a few days at Resolute Bay. Todd Gore, the manager of the aircraft company that was going to fly us to Ward Hunt Island, had relentlessly baited Mo and she had decided to have her revenge. One evening, while he was away, she went into his room armed with a vacuum cleaner and several pounds of flour. First she reversed the polarity on the vacuum to make it blow rather than suck and then she filled the cylinder. She hid the machine in the wardrobe and wired it into the switch of his bedside lamp. The results were spectacular. Todd returned from an evening at the local bar, pretty much the worse for wear, and went to bed. The shouts and bangs that followed quickly told us that Mo's trick had worked a treat. All was confirmed when a snow-white Todd came reeling from his room, enveloped in a large white cloud.

We would eat when the radio call was over, taking it in turn, spoon by spoon, to dip in the pot between us. After eating, we made any repairs that were necessary, and there would be a final hot chocolate drink. Often I yearned for something good to read but books had been banished along with other excess weight. This was perhaps a serious mistake for here was the time I'd always lacked for tackling Proust. A paperback edition of *War and Peace* might have paid incalculable dividends in terms of morale if only we had been prepared to sacrifice one day's ration each. Think of all that butter and fuel we had thrown out in the early days! Even a Le Carré thriller would have provided something better to think about during the long hours of manhauling than a repetitive song about chickens. Instead we settled for sleep between eleven and twelve o'clock. It was much the same for day after day after day.

NINE

★

Sea of Glass

EATING MORE did help to make us brighter, but the hunger still grew steadily worse and, with the weight loss we had already sustained, we became very cold. The season was advancing, and once the effect of breakfast had worn off, the chill permeated our bodies. It became a constant battle to maintain our core temperature and especially to keep our hands and feet functioning. One of the worst effects was that you wanted to pee a lot, and one of the prerequisites of peeing was that you had to take your mitts off to undo zips. While you stood there for just those few seconds, your fingers became painful and then useless, and when you had finished, you couldn't get your mitts on again. For some reason you also couldn't finish peeing successfully. All men recognise the 'last drip down the leg' phenomenon, but here it was the last half cupful. I constantly had that horrible feeling of warm wetness down the leg that quickly turned to ice. Later, in the tent, the urine-soaked clothing irritated the skin, and stank. Mind you, after a couple of months without washing we stank anyway and lived with it.

Our altitude increased, and we went through ten thousand and then eleven thousand feet. The thin air made the hauling harder and somehow the cold more piercing. When I read in Messner's account that he had felt the effects of the altitude on the plateau, I was very dubious. I had assumed that he was just putting it in for effect, especially as he had been to the top of Everest without oxygen and so must be pretty immune to the minimal effects of the altitudes we were facing. I was surprised when we felt it so badly. Later I learned the reason why. At high latitudes the air pressure is less than it is at the Equator.

134

Our height of close to 11,000 feet was therefore the equivalent of more like 14,000 feet in the Alps. It would not be surprising if we felt breathless pulling heavy loads near the top of Mont Blanc.

Yet, despite the hunger, the cold and the altitude, the days went by and our tally went steadily through the seventies. The wind still didn't come, and we pulled eleven or twelve miles in a similar number of hours. Desperately slowly we crawled over the bleak plain and the Pole receded. As it did so, my mornings of darkness decreased and I found the prospect of the journey ahead a little easier to take. For the first time I could glimpse a small light at the end of the tunnel. It was a long, long way off but it was a bright dot. There would even be some light before we got to it. When we reached the mountains we would have something to distract us; obstacles, crevasses, blue-ice, beauty. Anything would be better than where we were. We would pass beyond the white emptiness, and the days would surely improve. I began to believe that I would fulfil my dream of seeing the Beardmore Glacier, even if the wind never blew.

Every day I said to myself, 'I must remember this. I must never forget how awful it has been.' Yet these thoughts I stored for the future, for now I could keep going. Things had changed since the days when I had planned my brain haemorrhage.

I worried about Ran's foot. Although I tried treating it with antibiotics and anti-inflammatories, they hardly helped, and it began to look as if this might be our undoing. We talked about it often.

'How does it look?' asked Ran.

'To use a medical term, bloody awful,' I replied. 'It could blow up at any time, and I've tried everything that we've got to treat it. My guess is that it's refreezing every day and that by now the infection may have got into the bone. It really is a considerable risk.'

'Will it last?'

'I don't know. I would guess it's about fifty fifty.'

'Listen. If you get this foot to the Gate, I'll buy you a meal at Simpson's. It's not a bet, just a plea.'

Ran liked this sort of arrangement – a bet against fate. He also liked regular bets. I had already won £5 for Clinton

becoming U.S. President and a meal at Overton's for pre-
dicting on I think it was Day 30 that we would reach the
Pole before midnight on Day 68. Ran had won a breakfast
at Claridges for spotting the Pole station first, and was later
to win a slap-up meal on the way home. Eventually we were
to leave Antarctica evens.

'You're on,' I said, 'but somehow I don't think it's in
my hands.'

On Days 80 and 81 my prayers were answered and we
finally got some wind from the south. We made good distances, but on each occasion the wind was building while we
moved and before long it became too strong to go on with
safety. Unfortunately we didn't decide to stop early enough.
Instead we allowed ourselves to be dragged through belts of
sastrugi at dangerously fast speeds. Frequently, the sledges
turned over and were ripped along upside down. They either
righted themselves or we released the control lines and stopped.
The hammering we were giving ourselves and our kit was
worrying. As before, the sails also caught on ice obstacles
and often became tangled, but now it was much colder and
the forced delays, messing about stationary in the wind, were
bound to damage our hands and feet. We got away with it on
Day 80, but on the following day we paid the price. We had
just decided that it was too risky to continue when I looked
back at my sledge with horror. I could remember tying my
two ski-sticks on the top before starting. I had even used three
cross-straps instead of two, realising the need for extra care.

'Ran, my sticks! They've gone!'

'What do you mean, gone? They can't have.'

'But I tell you they have. They must have been ripped off
when my sledge turned over. I'm going back to look for them.'

'Don't be ridiculous,' he snapped. 'They could be anywhere.'

'You don't have to come,' I said. 'You can put up the
tent here, and I'll head back following my tracks. I'll take
a bit of kit in my rucksack for safety. Even if it takes a
day, it will be worth it. There's no way I can pull without
sticks.'

'Mike, you can have one of mine, or both if necessary.
They could be miles away, and in some areas the tracks will

be blown out. You might not find them, nor your way back here. It would be suicidal.'

He spoke sense. My idea was stupid. I just had to live with it. As for his offer to share his sticks, I was very grateful. I'm not sure I would have done the same. Pulling with one stick would be very difficult. At least it would for me. Being so light, I had always relied on adding upper body power to pull the sledge. Ran, on the other hand, had used the sticks simply for rhythm. Perhaps he wouldn't be greatly affected by having only one.

We packed away the chutes and set off pulling. The wind was still howling at our backs. It was so frustrating to have it blow in the right direction without being able to use it. As I walked I found that I had another problem which had resulted from our lightweight ski-bindings having no emergency release mechanism, unlike those used in the downhill sport. My foot had been clamped firmly to a six-foot board when I had fallen backwards and wrenched the front of my ankle hard. At first I thought it was mildly sprained and was surprised to find it getting steadily worse. It was not until well after my return to Britain, when it was still bothering me, that I discovered that the tear had been strong enough to rip off a fragment of bone at the lower end of my tibia. Until then I had not considered a fracture.

My hands were also bad. The untangling of the chutes with either bare or thinly gloved fingers had led to frostbite. Nine out of ten of them were blistered and swollen, and very painful. Ran's fingers had escaped, partly because he was better than I was at preventing his chute from tangling on obstructions and partly because, if it did get tangled, he was worse than I at undoing it. When it got into a real state, he always asked for my help. His feet, however, were another matter. The trouble was that sailing at this altitude was a bitterly cold experience and his hard plastic boots did nothing to protect his toes. We had had to choose the footwear *because* of the sailing. A rigid boot was essential if it was to be used with a binding that clamped down at the heel. He had poorer peripheral circulation than I, due partly to his age, but also to his having been a smoker. The long-standing damage around the old graft on the right foot was now worse than ever, and an area around it had become horribly mottled. He also had frostbite on the tips of some other toes on that foot. His left foot, however, was the more shocking. There all the toes had blackened ends and clearly a couple had been deeply frozen. He was now in real trouble. Not only were they likely to become infected, they were going to give him hell, and he was likely to lose one or more.

Our stop also revealed breakages inside my sledge. Just as with the ski-sticks, I had been aware when I packed it that the sailing might cause damage and so I had carefully laid the satellite beacon on top of my sleeping bag, wedged in on either side by other soft items. I had not anticipated that the thermos flask, placed several feet away at the rear of the sledge, would become a free-ranging agent. When I opened the cover, it was evident that this eight-pound solid chunk had been flying around the interior as the sledge bumped over the ice ridges. With dismay, I saw that it had smashed the antenna of the satellite beacon. This loss was very serious. It left us totally reliant on one radio when it came to calling for an aircraft. If we were going to cut it fine on food supplies, it would have been nice to know that we had a back-up communications system. I took it apart with the Swiss Army knife but couldn't repair it. The next day, we also found that the thermos itself was useless. We were down to two flasks which didn't work, and since wrapping them in a sleeping bag only kept them warm for long enough for one to be used, it effectively meant only one soup a day. The sailing had gained us many miles, but it was at considerable cost.

On Day 82, as once more we hauled the sledges, Ran suddenly stopped.

'Mike ... Mike, look!'

I looked in the direction towards which he was pointing and at first saw nothing. Then I spotted them and involuntarily cried out, not quietly, but in a loud, joyous, unselfconscious whoop. Far in the distance, lying slightly to the right of our course were some mountains – distant flecks of grey, breaking the white horizon for the first time since those tiny triangular peaks two months earlier. It seemed likely that these were the nunataks that lay off Mount Ward, the mountain that Charles

Swithinbank had identified as the best point at which to enter
the glacier system. We consulted the map, and changed course
slightly to head towards them. Our speed increased as, buoyed
up by the sight of a target, our morale lifted. Over the course
of the day they came nearer and nearer. Another stage of our
journey was ending and it looked as if we might even leave
the plateau before we cut back on our food.

That night we camped just a few miles from the nearest
peak and confirmed our position. Unlike Scott, it was our aim
to reach the Beardmore Glacier by using a large tributary called
the Mill. This would take us round the very upper part of the
Beardmore, which was notorious for ice falls and crevassing.
To enter the Mill system, we needed to pass between an out-
lying peak to the east and Mount Ward to the west, but when
we approached the mountains the next day, there seemed to
be a number of possible choices that fitted the features that
Swithinbank had described. Eventually we committed ourselves mistakenly to passing west of Mount Ward, although this
didn't become apparent until we had travelled several miles
along the wrong route. It didn't matter. By the time we realised our mistake, it was obvious that we could descend just
as easily where we were. The flat plain had gradually begun
to slope. Then the surface changed from white wind-blown
snow to grey, and then blue-ice. When we moved in between
the mountains, it was as if we reached a weir, the place where
the ice of the plateau flooded into the small unnamed tributary.
Quite suddenly it became very steep, and the sledges began to
slide freely. Soon we were almost running. Like the ice itself,
we began to flow down the hill, poured from the plateau into
the glacier system.

All told, we had dropped a thousand feet when we set up
the tent in the middle of two ice rivers which fused to form the
Mill itself. Already it was two or three miles wide, a scale that
left me dumb. I had seen glaciers in the Alps, the Himalayas,
the Andes, and elsewhere in Antarctica, but these exceeded all
my expectations. Somehow I had come to believe that when
we came to Mount Ward and looked down the glacier system,
I would be able to see in the far distance the far side of the
mountain range and the ice-shelf to which the glaciers were

all flowing. Of course, if I had consulted the map properly, I would have realised that the shelf was well over 140 miles away and 10,000 feet below us. Clearly it would be impossible to see that far even from the very top of the mountains, but I hadn't registered this.

About two miles away, below our tiny camp, our tributary met the other in a turmoil of heavily crevassed blue-ice. Then the Mill itself rolled into the distance before disappearing around a far corner. The whole flow was dominated by huge mountain massifs, large enough to be ranges in themselves, and in the direction from which we had come I could see the ice of the plateau, spilling over the edge in places, to feed the vast frozen network. To east and west there was more, and the plateau edge receded to infinity, glinting occasionally in the low light. To the north, the mountains seemed to continue for ever, rank upon rank of giant peaks that ranged in colour from a pale blue, to rust reds and blacks. The place was glorious, and it made the whole journey seem worthwhile. We felt that we had just left the very roof of the world, and I could see the lines of longitude descending, radiating, and spreading through the mountains. Beyond, they travelled across the sea, getting wider and wider, until eventually every land on earth lay between them. We stood close to the source of everything – close to the point of creation.

We were in the midst of a sea of gleaming glass. It shone in every direction – white, blue, green, an ocean of translucence. It was diamond hard, yet it was not smooth. Instead it was choppy, rippled, filled with motionless waves, water vitrified during a violent squall. For us, the roughness was a godsend. Even with the scalloped ripples it was incredibly slippery, and where smooth it was virtually uncrossable.

When we had started out, we had known that we would meet areas like this but had not anticipated so many. With the dreadful weights we were to pull, carrying crampons had seemed like a luxury. Reckoning that he could improvise grips, Ran spent the evenings before we reached the mountains in the vain attempt. At first he cut up used fuel bottles to make metal spikes which he hoped we could tie on with paracord, but the metal was too soft, and with our weight on them, the spikes were instantly flattened and useless. Undeterred, he set about fashioning some rope grips, spending hours knotting, sewing and affixing straps. In the end he was rightfully proud of his beautiful creations, and they could even be put on and taken off easily. Although they would have been helpful in some circumstances, here the thick cords that passed under both the toe and heel of the boot made no discernible difference. The ice was far too hard, and all his efforts had come to nought. We just had to live with it being slippery and be thankful that the scalloped effect at least allowed our boots some traction. With the help of our one ski-stick each, we could just maintain our balance. Meanwhile, we worked on creating second ski-sticks by cutting up our spare ski.

If retaining grip on the ice was difficult on gentle inclines, it became impossible when on any real slope. Then, even if the feet gripped, the sledges would pick up speed and either knock us over from behind or go past on the downhill side to twist us round and pull us over. We had countless falls on the hard ridged surface, and it was never clear what hurt the most. When your feet slipped from under you, you came down fast with all your weight, and whatever bore the brunt of the fall let you know about it. At the same time, reflexes whipped out a hand with the intention of breaking the fall, but the result was simply that frost-damaged fingers added their scream to the pain. In addition, my ankle gave further vicious stabs. Fractures hurt and are not to be walked on. The combination of signals had me crying out and my cheeks were streaked with tears.

Ran had been getting farther and farther ahead as my ankle had begun to make itself painfully felt. With every step that we descended, the cracked bone moved, grating inside the swollen joint. When going downhill, the sole of the foot lands at an angle and the ligaments at the front of the ankle are put under strain. These ligaments were joined to the broken flake and every pace from ten thousand feet to sea level was going to be hell. I would be slowed from top to bottom of the one hundred and fifty mile glacier.

While I was being held back by the pain, Ran now found his sledge running freely on the ice and began to take advantage of his long legs. He started to move at considerable speed, encouraged to do so by the slippery surfaces. It was easier for him to progress in a teetering run, rather than try to control his speed, and with a constant wind blowing down the valleys, he also found it very cold unless he hurried. The wind came from the cold air of the plateau behind us. Flowing over those broad weirs of ice that marked the edge, it accelerated as it began to drop rapidly and was then channelled by the mountain massifs to become faster still before it screamed through the ice-carved valleys, carrying all before it. The wind was the cause of the bare blue-ice on which we walked, blasting it clean and racing onwards laden with snow and ice. Our clothing was laughable in the face of such a catabatic gale. That icy wind cut through to the skin with no hindrance. It was as if we were naked, and it hurt. It hurt from the start to the finish of each day.

Ran was a small orange dot and I despised him with all my heart. He had never fallen so far behind when I had been the faster. I would always stop and wait at each of our changeovers. Admittedly he had asked me if I minded dropping the alternation system; he found it too cold to wait. I had said that I didn't and apologised for my slowness, due to both my ankle, and my height. Even if I had been fine, there was no way that anyone of five-foot-seven could have kept up with a half-striding, half-running man of six-foot-two. I had thought that I was agreeing to let him choose his moments for stopping, I didn't expect him almost to disappear. It was bloody stupid; he would have to wait in the end anyway. It was also madness when the weather conditions were such that visibility could close down at any moment. There were no tracks to follow and I could easily lose him. Stumbling along behind, cursing him constantly, I was feeling the demoralisation that he must have experienced for most of our long journey.

At last he waited. He realised that the blowing snow was a danger and had no choice. By the time I joined him he was visibly shivering and there was fury written on his features.

'Can't you go any faster,' he said aggressively.

'No I damn well can't,' I replied. 'I'm going as fast as I can.'

'Well try to keep close. It's too cold to wait and things are getting bad. We've got to find somewhere to camp where there's a little shelter. We'd never be able to pitch the tent in this. I doubt that we could even get the ice-screws in.'

It was true. The tent would be almost uncontrollable in the wind, and even if we could hold it down, the ridged blue-ice would be brittle as well as hard and would shatter rather than take our ice-screws. It was also too steep for a tent, but I was getting tired and couldn't take much more.

'Does anywhere on the map look likely?' I asked.

'No, not for quite a way. The ice abuts directly against the cliff for a considerable distance, and there's certainly no way through out there.' He pointed towards the centre of the glacier, a broken chaos of ice cliffs and caverns. 'About five or six miles down, there's a small peninsular of rock jutting out. Perhaps we can get into the lee of that and find some drifted snow for a camp.'

Christ! Five or six miles more? I didn't feel as if I could make one. We'd already been going for ten hours and walking with my damned ankle was so wearing. Had Ran really lived with pain like this for all those weeks? I didn't know. I had no way of making a comparison. He seemed to be having few problems now.

'I guess we have no option,' I said. 'Let's get on with it. But don't expect me to go fast. I'm not having you on. I'm shorter than you, I'm knackered, and my ankle hurts like hell. I'm afraid you're just going to have to wait, cold or not.'

That evening became horrendous. The wind increased until it howled around us and the air was thick with sharp shards of ice. Even small stones were flying, striking our legs as we walked, battering our faces if we lifted our eyes from the ground. I stumbled on, head down and back hunched against the onslaught, slipping, falling, cursing, crying. The blue-ice rose, and fell, and rolled on downwards – a desperate surface punctuated by deep crevasses that loomed out of the mist, then disappeared as quickly as they came. Beside us, the west bank of the glacier met an enormous cliff, a towering wall of massively layered sandstone - rust reds, rich browns, coal blacks. It could have been beautiful in other circumstances, but now the unbroken line trapped us in the maelstrom. We were pinned against the cliff by the waves of crevasses further out and the rising tide of the furious wind. Blindly, we swam on, seeking a beach, a harbour of safety. There was none. We just went on and on.

Ran still went too quickly for me, turning frequently to stare, beckon, or call, his futile words whipped instantly away. I suppose he did it either to encourage or press me on, but when I saw that waving arm or read those soundless lips, the anger rose within me.

'You wait!' I hissed. 'You wait until my ankle's better and we're on the flat. Then you'll see some beckoning. Bastard!'

Eleven hours, then twelve passed, and on we struggled, sick with fatigue. I could no longer think clearly and my legs were crying out for respite. I was staggering, weaving from side to side while trying to follow Ran's tenuous trail. It came and went with the gusts of wind, as did his shadowy figure, although he was now careful not to let me drop behind. A part of me kept saying 'Stop ... Sit down ... Take a rest. It doesn't matter if you wait a while just here.' But sense prevailed, fought back and answered, 'No ... go on ... it cannot be far now.' Finally, after nearly fourteen hours of savagery, we saw a dark promontory of rock jutting into the ice flow just ahead. Around it, the glacier was contorted and broken, but with care we threaded a route through the reefs and entered our long-sought haven, a place where we could anchor our tent and weather out the storm.

All around us there were rocks, the first we had seen and touched since we had left South America nearly three months before. They were of all sizes, shapes and colours, and were strewn about our little enclave. Nowhere was flat, and so we set our tent between two massive boulders, protected from the wind by the earth itself. Around us the storm still ebbed and flowed, now quiet, then shrieking and, occasionally, with small tornado-like columns of ice crystals spiralling round our shelter like evil wraiths. The boulders among which we camped had fallen from the steep cliff above us, but although we lay close in beneath it, we ignored the danger. Rest was taken gratefully, and to us our tent was the safest place on earth.

TEN

★

Bearding the Beardmore

THE CUTTING was so slow. A Swiss Army knife was just not the right tool for the job. After I had managed to remove the ski-binding – not easy when I couldn't undo the screws and had to jemmy it off with an ice axe – I had started to cut the spare ski in half lengthways, with the aim of creating two new ski-sticks. In the core was a metal plate, and so the job entailed using a three-inch hacksaw blade to cut through more than six feet of tough metal-reinforced laminate. I was now into my third evening of cutting and had yet to reach halfway. Still, they would be ready for the end of the glacier, a bit late to help us with the blue-ice and the slopes but better late than never. The job was ruining my hands. Since the damage on those days of sailing, they had become much worse. Every finger was a mess where the original numb whiteness had become a horribly swollen blister, and these wept pus which dripped on to everything. I had even coated the pages of my diary, which then stuck together. Not that I was able to write much any more. Holding a pen was near impossible. I covered the fingers in dressings, but by the end of each day the pus had seeped through and adhered to my gloves. Sometimes it took over half an hour of coaxing before I was in a position to make the final wrench which would rip the skin off to expose thin raw digits beneath.

The skinless fingers were extremely sensitive, and there was nothing I could do to protect them. Even the nails came off, and every task became a torment. Dressing in the morning, cooking, walking, all were conducted with pain, and any task which entailed removing gloves became a trial. This particularly applied to having a pee. I found myself crying as I tried to handle zips, and then crying again when I tried to push my deformed hands back into my mitts. Even at night there was no escape. My hands inadvertently brushed the inside of my bag. I lay sleepless with the pain.

There was another reason for my insomnia, I had become too hungry. We had been on half rations since the day we entered the glacier system. Our evening meal was pitifully small, just a few spoonfuls each and the pot was empty, leaving an almost painful void in shrunken stomachs that called for more. There was none, and so food came to dominate my thinking. When I tried to get some sleep, it was in part for rest and escape from pain, but my chief thought as I lay down was that a few hours unconscious would bring the breakfast nearer. A few hours? I was grateful for a few minutes! Lying in my bag on a fleshless spine, I examined my own body. Everywhere the bones protruded and my abdomen was sunken. My legs were thin as an old man's, wasted and weak. Could these inadequate excuses for limbs carry me much further? I was beginning to doubt it on such a pathetic intake. During the day, we were down to two tiny chocolate bars and one thermos of soup between us. We stopped only once, for just a few minutes, during the whole of our twelve-hour days. It was too much to ask of our now frail bodies. Even the bottom of the glacier was questionable; beyond must be impossible.

Beside me, Ran was also awake. His feet had deteriorated and new damage from the sailing had blistered and was breaking open. Although, they scarcely slowed him in the day, it was probably because his toes refroze and he couldn't feel them. At night, they drove him to distraction, the pain becoming worse as they warmed inside his sleeping bag. Often, within half an hour of getting into our bags, the throbbing would drive him out. He sat upright, trying to cool his feet to gain relief. Later I would doze fitfully, restless on the hard ice surface, and woken repeatedly by stabs of pain from my hands. Each time I awoke, he would still be there, unable to gain the rest that he needed so badly, writing more in his diary to distract himself. If he saw my eyes open, he would talk, glad to share his wakefulness. In the morning, black-eyed after the long night, he would tell me his latest plans and worries for the future – everything from the menus for meals with Ginny to the jobs he might do now that his exploring days were over.

'This is the last, Mike. I shan't be going away again. It's all been too nasty. The whole thing has been spoiled by my foot and by my getting too old. Even though we might make it to the shelf, I should have never come in the first place.'

'What rubbish,' I said. 'Your foot, I can understand, but your age problem is in your head. It's *me* holding *you* up, remember.'

I glanced at him. He did look old, thin and haggard. Perched upon his bony buttocks, his long legs stretched in front of him were worse than mine, and they ended in those horribly damaged feet. His face was ravaged, almost ancient, and hooded lids covered eyes that were somehow dulled. His features were puffed and doughy, and his lips were still scabbed and broken in places. The frost had left its mark. His ears were blistered and beneath one eye was a raw patch where he'd pulled off glasses while they were still frozen on. His hair, thinning a little before we started, was now falling out in tufts. Somehow it got into our food, into drinks, into everything. Not that it was just *his* hair; mine was also coming out. I sighed. I probably looked as bad as he did. We had no mirror and I hadn't seen my face for nearly three months. I wondered how much of this unnatural ageing would be permanent. I used to look much younger than my age. Several times when I worked as a hospital doctor it led to comment.

The last I could recall was shortly before we went to Siberia and the north. I was working as a medical registrar at St Thomas's Hospital in London, and on that particular evening was the acting 'Resident Assistant Physician'. From the medical as opposed to surgical point of view, I was the most senior doctor on the hospital site, with the immediate responsibility for hundreds of patients and beds. A woman arrived in casualty with pneumonia. She was sick but quite alert, and I decided that she needed admission. I took a full history, thoroughly examined her, and even took blood for tests rather than disturb my houseman or the senior houseman who were busy elsewhere. Finally I explained to her the nature of her problem and told her what would happen and to which ward she would be going. 'Thank you dear,' she said. 'Will I be seeing the proper doctor there?'

'The trouble is,' Ran continued, 'that I can't do anything. I don't have any qualifications or skills and I need a steady income for a few more years.'

'What about your writing?' I said. 'That's done you pretty well, and you'll get a book out of this trip, and then there's the novel you were talking about. You're easily good enough to do it full time.'

'No, it's not reliable enough,' he replied. 'I need a job with a regular income until I get my writing more established. I'm thinking of becoming a waiter at Claridges.'

'You are joking!' I exclaimed.

'No, I'm not. I used to go in there a lot when I worked for Oxy. They do incredibly well. You can get more than £30,000 for a few months in the summer. The head waiter told me so. I know him well.'

The pay seemed unlikely, but no doubt Ran did know the staff. After the Transglobe expedition, he had landed himself a job as public relations consultant for Dr Armand Hammer, the multi-millionaire owner of Occidental oil. He worked mainly on a personal level rather than for the company itself, helping particularly with Hammer's philanthropic ventures that were linked to Prince Charles. Whenever Hammer was in London, he would take over an entire floor at Claridges and Ran always organised it and stayed with him. No, there might be some exaggeration, but the basis would lie in truth.

'Ran, they wouldn't take you on. You've got no experience. Besides, the press would crucify you. You'd never live it down.'

'I don't care,' he said. 'I've go to do something, and I can't think of anything else. Anyway, first things first. We've got to finish this yet, and the way my foot's been feeling, I don't know if I can.'

I looked at his feet. They were a ghastly sight. The right foot was deformed by the swelling at the base of the little toe, a product of two months of inflammation and infection, and some of the other toes were blackened and blistered. The left was far worse. Where once had been his toes, there were now black fluid-filled bags, so grotesquely swollen that they merged into one. From them oozed a vile dark liquid that smelt dreadful, despite the cold.

'They're certainly bad,' I said, 'and getting worse by the day. You can only walk on them because they freeze. I don't think the antibiotics are controlling the infection, and we're nearly out of them anyway. I'd be lying if I told you there was no risk. These need proper attention, in a hospital.'

I paused for a moment and then added softly, 'I'd understand if you felt we had to stop.'

'Just get me to the Gate,' he replied. 'That will be success, and then we can talk of going on.'

It was our fourth afternoon in the mountains, and we were nearly down the Mill. The gradients had eased, and although it was uncomfortable, I was moving much faster. Ran was still running ahead, though that was up to him. It was still windy and cold, but visibility was good. Ahead I could see the junction of the Mill and the Beardmore at Plunkett point. I felt much happier than I'd been for the last few days, chiefly because the pain was easier. It was a shame we couldn't sail. The wind dropped a little, and if the surface had been softer it might have been possible. Maybe we'd be able to use the sails on the glacier itself, once we got out to the middle where it was said to be crevasse-free.

The glacier was so huge I could scarcely credit it. Up to the left, high above us and fifty miles away, we could see its source at the lip of the Polar plateau. From there it flowed down to pour over the Shackleton ice falls, the enormous barrier which had proved so difficult for the earlier expeditions and which we had taken the Mill to avoid. Further down it widened, and in front of us it was nearly thirty miles across – wider than Europe's largest glacier is long. The whole thing was constructed of parallel bands of different shaded ice, each a tributary that joined further up its course. Associated with many of these bands were moraines – ridges of rock-strewn ice that formed at the sides of the glaciers where they ground away the substance of the mountains. Where tributaries merged, the

149

moraines merged too, and the lateral dirt bands became central markings. The glacier ended up vividly striped, each band the ice from a different source. Even at this distance, I could see that some of the ice bands were free of cracks, whereas others were riven through and through. Our aim was to find a safe line and follow it far enough to reach the lower glacier system. There, where the catabatic winds were less violent, the crevasses should all be bridged, and we would emerge on to a great white and featureless river, meandering powerfully to the end of the mountains, the edge of the continent.

Ahead, I saw Ran stop, and guessed he was thinking of making camp. He was probably waiting for me to join him before selecting a spot. We would have to seek some drift among the crevasses and folds. We were still on the wretched blue-ice and finding a campsite was difficult. Still, at least the sledge now moved easily. I hurried on towards him. It hurt when I went too fast and I fell a couple of times and had to ease back a little. I smiled as I drew up to Ran.

'Thanks for waiting. I'm sorry I'm going slowly, but we've done well. I should think it's our best day yet.'

His response caught me unawares.

'Is there anything the matter?' he said with a note of false concern. It reminded me of my words months earlier.

'No,' I replied, puzzled. 'My ankle still hurts, and I'm beginning to wonder if it's actually broken, but the pain's manageable now the terrain's eased off.'

'Then why are you going unbelievably slowly?' he said harshly. 'You've just got to go faster.'

I snapped. I had never urged him to go faster, and the only time that I had ever criticised him was after the business of giving Kagge our position, when he had done his leader bit.

'Damn you!' I spat. 'I don't have to bloody well do anything. I'm not going unbelievably slowly, you are going unbelievably fast. At times you're nearly running. Can't you see that?'

'No, I can't,' he said irritably. 'But in any case, if I don't keep moving I can't keep warm. Here, take this ski-stick as well. Use both, it might help.'

He handed me the other ski-stick and turned and was off.

26 Approaching Mount Kyffin

27 The Gateway, from the slopes of Mount Hope

28 Black dots at the end of the longest unbroken trail in history

29 Ran and Mike, down and out at the Ross ice-shelf pick-up

I was seething. He seemed to think that I wasn't making an effort, but I was, and I resented his criticism. I wished I'd rubbed his nose in it when he'd held things up for two months.

Still, I was thankful for the extra stick. Having two supports made a world of difference, and I could walk more steadily without the risk of falling. How he managed to walk without ski-sticks at all, I don't know, but he did, and he still went faster than I could.

In the tent that night I couldn't hide my smug delight when I read out our position from the Magellan. We had made well over twenty miles, by far the greatest distance we had travelled in a day without sailing. It vindicated my speed. I had been right and we had both been moving fast.

The following day we got on to the Beardmore itself and were dwarfed. For a couple of hours we tried to take a route along the side of the huge glacier, hoping to take the shortest line, but there were crevasses everywhere and we were forced to turn out towards the middle of the river of ice. There the going was easier, and with the gradients much gentler, and the ice now covered by a layer of soft snow, the sledges began dragging again. My problem with Ran's speed was lessened. We resumed the system of alternating leads and for the next couple of days it was back to a desperate slog.

With the extra work, we became hungrier than ever, and with the hunger the last remnants of self-control disappeared. Throughout the trip the chocolate bars had been our heaven, and for most of it we had eaten one in the morning with coffee, two during the day, and one in the evening with tea. When we were reduced to two, there was a dilemma. Did we eat them in the morning and day, or try to keep them for the evening? Now it was out of our hands. The drive to eat was too great. When we took the chocolate from the ration packs in the morning and put it in our pockets, it was going to be eaten soon, however stupid that might be. The temptation of knowing it was there was quite beyond us, and before we had completed an hour, often before we had left the tent, we had devoured the lot. It was the only way to deal with it, and it was strangely satisfying. Only when they were gone could you free yourself of torment.

Freedom from torment did not mean peace of mind. Thoughts of food now dominated my day as well as my night and I was back to living in day-dreams, but the dreams had a strange quality. The thoughts during the first month of our journey, those constructive ideas about all the things that I would do at home, had been sharp and clear, quite distinct from reality. Even in the second month, when the ideas had run out and my mind had been filled with black shadows of defeat, circles of logistics, Scott or just inanity, the thoughts had still been delineated from the sledging. Now, with the constant hunger and the craving for food, I seemed to drift in and out of true consciousness, lost in a jumbled continuum of meals that floated through the real world. My family waited at the end of the glacier, where Heathrow's Terminal Four stood under Mount Hope and my mother organised the catering. I ate cake with the children in the Wendy house while sitting on my sledge and drinking fatty soup through an iced balaclava. Out for a day's hike, I followed my father into a country pub, but couldn't understand why he was dragging something. Often, there was the feeling that others journeyed with us. The boundary between thought and reality had blurred and for much of the day I inhabited a shadowy world of both.

Ran was also obsessed, and although I couldn't read his day-dreams, he wrote of food and little else. In his diary, day after day, he would expand a massively imaginative menu he planned to sit down and eat with Ginny when he got back to his farm on Exmoor. It ran into course after course, and finally occupied several pages of tiny script. It was a totally unrealistic fantasy of what he intended to devour in one sitting, although previously, one almost as complex had eventually come to fruition. After our return from the Arctic a bemused Ginny had actually been presented with a fifteen course-meal.

Our journey continued. Not far ahead, we could see where the glacier narrowed to run between The Cloudmaker and Wedge Face and almost imperceptibly we crept towards this constriction. Soon we would have to round the crevasse field generated by Wedge Face itself – an upheaval in the ice caused by the glacier flowing past the mountain that jutted into the ice stream. Our maps clearly indicated that before we reached it we should move to the left, or western side of the glacier, and Charles Swithinbank had said the same. There we should meet only minor disruption, and so gradually we moved farther and farther into mid-stream.

At the same time, we became slower and slower. Well over a thousand miles lay behind us, and our bodies had paid the price. The sledges now weighed less than two hundred pounds but they were dead weights; it was as if we hauled logs through sand. Even though we were on flattish ground, the snow cover reduced us to a crawl and we were crushed by fatigue. I watched Ran ahead of me, bowed by the load. He was all angles, and his clothes hung half empty. He was cachectic, like a man with a terminal illness. I had seen such patients – strong men reduced to skin-covered bone by tumours growing wildly inside them. We were the same. Along with our fat, we had lost most of our muscles, burned as fuel to feed their own efforts. There was no doubt that we were severely debilitated and close to our limits. It wouldn't be much longer until we could pull no more. It was not just a question of will; whatever our determination, we would reach a time when we would slow to a halt. Even the magnificent mountains on either side could not lift us to go faster and defeat seemed increasingly possible.

Then things changed.

For the first time since entering the glacier system, the icy blast from the plateau decreased to the extent that it became manageable for sailing. It wasn't blowing straight down the glacier, and if we sailed, it would carry us in towards Wedge Face, but we couldn't resist a chance to move a few miles at less dreadful cost. Wedge Face was still more than ten miles distant and, knowing our luck, we would get no more than a short ride. Then we could angle out again to pass the crevasse field. Even if the wind continued, the mountain itself might turn it, allowing us to sail outwards again.

We got out the chutes and moved off. Here on the smooth soft snow, with no sastrugi, it was all so much easier than it had been the couple of times before. We raced along, the skis swishing through two-inches of shimmering crystals, only the ski-tips showing as they hissed through the soft white blanket. We were exhilarated, and caution was literally thrown to the wind as the black cliff of Wedge Face drew nearer. Finally, instead of dying, the wind became too strong and we had to stop for our own safety, but we had been blown along for more than an hour, and had saved nearly a whole day's travel. We were thrilled, but not for long.

By the time we had put the chutes away visibility had become very limited. Loose snow was being driven along the surface, obscuring everything up to a height of about ten feet. Above, the sky was a deep blue, and the mountain peaks on the far side of the glacier gleamed in low orange sunlight, topped by nacreous clouds. Towering over us, blotting out a whole quadrant of the sky, rose the massive bulk of the darkly shadowed hanging cliff of Wedge Face. We started walking south-west with a view to rounding the mountain and, we hoped, the crevasse field as well. The wind was at least force ten and the spindrift swept and swirled around us, hissing along and hiding the ground ahead.

Suddenly we both saw it, right in our path. There, rising out of the blowing mist, was an enormous hump-back of fragmented, disrupted and tortuous ice. It must have risen to a hundred feet and extended away to our left as far as we could see. We stopped and looked, wondering what to do. Either we had to make a massive diversion to avoid it or we took it on direct. It would be slow to cross, but the direct approach must save time. We plumped for the frontal assault and began to climb.

The slope rose steadily, broken by huge cracks, most of them running across our path and the line of the slope. This was to be expected, and by zig-zagging back and forth, we could find the places where the gaps narrowed and were bridged by snow. Slowly we climbed towards the middle of the disturbance. As we crossed the convexity we came to a region of total anarchy. The ice was split in all directions and it seemed as if more of the area was occupied by black voids than by white surface. Furthermore, most of the surface consisted of the wind-blasted blue glass, with just a few patches of soft snow which formed into crevasse bridges. It made things very difficult. It would have been suicidal to cross the bridges without skis, yet elsewhere they skittered sideways on the glassy surfaces which funnelled towards the deep canyons. Worse, the sledges had a mind of their own, slewing sideways at the least opportunity and doing their best to drag us to destruction. It was terrifying. At any time it seemed as if one could slip, fall or be pulled over, and nothing would have stopped one from disappearing through the gaping mouths, down into the dark black throats.

We made our way through like men in a maze, wandering back and forth, seeking bridges strong enough to bear us, and turning aside from chasms too large to cross. Our course meandered so much, and it would have been so cold if we delayed, that neither of us suggested using a rope. We just took our chances and looked for the routes that seemed strong. We both moved as fast as we could but Ran was once again hurrying, taking advantage of his height to heave his sledge up, down and round the obstacles. I followed more slowly, my ankle complaining bitterly at these new found inclines. I was back at a disadvantage and was not impressed by the return of intolerant glares and beckonings. Still, I was not quite so demoralised at being left behind and was indeed grateful to be there. At least everything I crossed Ran had crossed first, and with him being the heavier man, I thought I had a good chance of survival.

After almost four hours, in which we moved less than a mile, we began to descend slowly through a second area of simple transverse cracks to reach the flat ice on the other side. We had made it through. With the wind dying, the visibility improved and we could look to the north. Ahead, the huge river now seemed to be quite smooth, rolling only gently as it forged a last straight slash through the mountains. Far away to the right there was an unmistakable silhouette. Neither of us had ever seen it before but we both knew what it was. Rising vertically from the ice, a six thousand foot wall of red granite towered to a pointed summit. It was a peak out of Gormenghast, as unreal as a child's drawing. It was Mount Kyffin, the finger. Along with Mount Hope on the opposite side of the Beardmore Glacier, it pointed to the end of what was probably the final stage of our journey – the far side of the continent.

We camped that night beyond the crevasses. At the foot of the Wedge Face. Ensconced once more in our tiny shelter, we reviewed our situation.

'We've got nine and a half rations left,' I said. 'That's nineteen days if we leave no reserve at all. How long did Messner take from here?'

'About nineteen,' Ran replied, 'mainly sailing, but with some quite big hauling days. We could do it if we have the wind.'

'Maybe,' I responded, 'but only if we get more than he did. We're in no shape to make any big pulls, and there's also your feet. I don't suppose they would last.'

'It would have to be a raging infection to stop us getting to the main goal,' laughed Ran. 'I'm not intending to give up now.'

That was fair enough. We had come about thirteen hundred miles as the crow flies, and probably fifteen hundred in reality. To complete a crossing of the continent there were only thirty or so to go, but I wasn't sure that that was the main goal.

'And beyond the Gate?' I asked.

'That's more difficult,' he said, 'but I want to make the ice-shelf so, while there's still a chance, I think we should go for it. As long as you're ready to stop when the chance slips away.'

'That's fine by me,' I said. 'I realise that getting to Scott Base is pretty unlikely and I guess we'll just have to settle for the continent.'

'Well, don't sound so down about it,' Ran chided me. 'It's not a failure. We will have achieved something remarkable. I never reckoned we'd get anywhere near this far.'

'So why did you do it?' I asked. 'If you thought it was impossible, like I did, it couldn't have been for the money – that awful answer you give the press.'

'Yes, I suppose that's true,' he said thoughtfully. 'I'm not sure really, though money must be a big part of it because I wouldn't do it if it weren't my career.'

'Ah, but you chose your career, it didn't choose you,' I responded. 'You made it your living because you were good at the outdoor sort of things – winning biathlons, canoe instructor and all that. Because you were good at them, you

156

enjoyed them, or perhaps vice-versa. You must get some pleasure from these journeys.'

'I suppose I do,' he said quietly. 'Although this one has been pretty nasty. I'll admit that I enjoy talking about them afterwards, and I'm pleased to share them with the people that read the books or hear me speak. I'm also pleased that this will be a British success, but I won't start talking about the view or the philosophical stuff because, if I do, I'll be labelled a woolly-minded eccentric aristocrat. I'd rather the press said I was mercenary. At least everyone can relate to that.'

'Well, I think I'll relate to the woolly bits.' I smiled. 'And anyway, I thought you were French.'

Only one more obstacle lay between us and the completion of the crossing. Where the Beardmore flowed into the Ross ice-shelf, there would be another region of ice disruption, though there was a way past this one. When Shackleton pioneered the way south in 1908, and discovered the Beardmore, he found a safe entrance to the bottom end, the route he called 'the Gate'. It was a clever jink, taking the traveller behind Mount Hope and allowing him to slip past the area of major crevassing by using two minor valleys linked by a narrow col. All expeditions since have followed his path, and now we just had to reach that gateway, which we knew was marked by the Granite Towers.

On the following morning we set off. The sun was shining and the air was completely still. It was cold, about minus 40°C. The snow was sticky and the sledge heavy, and my back ached, but I felt renewed. To reach the Gate would be a triumph. Keep going and we would have done something special. Mount Kyffin helped. It grew larger and more glorious by the hour – a vertical marker at the peak of our horizontal mountain. The sight lifted me and my mind now pushed my feeble body. For the first time since before the mountains, I found the going easier than Ran. He had slowed, for even the end of the tunnel could not relieve the pain that rose to dominate his mind. He was hobbled and miserable, and I feared that the infection was finally taking off. But we made our requisite distance, and that night camped again, with less than twenty miles to go. It had been our ninetieth day of travel. Surely nothing could stop us now.

The next day, after a few hours' hauling, the air stirred once more. Then our hoods began to rustle as the white crystals kicked up by our skis started to flee before us. The wind became stronger, but it was intermittent and we went on hauling, thinking of the gusts as there to mock us. But they persisted. We opened our sails and were finally carried steadily forward, borne on the wind that for half our journey had been an enemy and for most of the rest an absent ally. It carried us the extra miles and soon, across the broadening frozen delta, we saw the Granite Towers and the entrance to our road. Suddenly it looked as if we could make it that day. We pressed on, not stopping for our tepid soup. As we drew closer, the Towers became greater, and what had appeared an ordinary broken cliff grew into huge red-granite pillars – a temple made for giants, a gateway to release.

There was a crevassed region at the foot of the Towers, where we had to stop sailing and move carefully. Slowly we crossed these last few mantraps, and as we did so, the monoliths slipped aside, and there before us lay our path. There were just a few hours more to go.

We approached the col together. It was so late in our evening that the sun was in the north, and we came up in deep shadow. Ahead, through the narrow saddle the sky was ablaze, and as we climbed those last few yards the grey unlit snow ignited round our feet. We reached the divide and stood in silence. Behind us the dark valley of our journey, three months of mental and physical hell, before us a sunlit world of freedom. A snow-covered slope, flanked by screes, dropped steeply to merge with the ice-shelf in another region of cracks. Further out there were more local disturbances but the eye didn't rest there. It was the world beyond that drew our gaze. The whole vastness of the Ross ice-shelf lay in front of us, stretching east, west, and north to the horizon. We had completed our journey. Whether we stopped here or carried on, this was the place that would mark our accomplishment. Here, and at that moment, we had reached the shore of the Pacific Ocean.

Ran smiled. I pushed back the tears. We shook hands.

'You owe me a meal at Simpson's,' I said.

ELEVEN

★

Beyond the Gate

OUR WORLD had changed. Around us there was nothing, no gate, no slope, no sea. The expanse to the north had disappeared in the mist. All was silence as we took down the tent and set off. We were back in the disorienting world of whiteout and almost without knowing it, certainly without sight, we completed the last few steps of our crossing and moved off the continent on to the Ross ice-shelf.

Our moment of triumph had been on the evening before, and now the weather seemed to mock us. The continent had disappeared and our journey was surely over. It seemed somehow pointless to wander off into the fog. What was there to be gained from going further? Why take the chance, the risk, the pain? For me the answer was simple – it was what I had set out to do. Maps always showed the ice-shelves in a different colour from the sea, and I wanted to draw a line that crossed the map from the blue on one side to the blue on the other. Only then would it match the journey proposed by Shackleton. All journeys before ours, except Messner's, had included those shelves, and I had no wish to break with tradition or reduce the scale of the challenge. I did not want to give up now and would cross the shelf as well if I possibly could.

We knew well that severe disruption and crevassing lay in front of us. Ran had plotted a route, working out distances and bearings from the maps, following Swithinbank's advice and using what he had seen from the Gate. Although now blind, he led the way forward, threading his way through the obstacles with confidence. It would take half a day to reach the relatively safe ice beyond.

159

It was very cold, and unlike up at the Gate, a stiff wind was blowing. It might have helped us if we could see, but even then, it would probably have been too dangerous to sail. Many hours passed as we hauled our way forward. Occasionally, through the gloom, huge areas of broken ice appeared, the ice thrown into turmoil by the inexorable forces of the Beardmore, creating havoc that spread for many miles. Each area of fragmentation had to be turned, and we hauled this way and that, making slow progress. We wished to head just west of north for Scott Base about four hundred miles away, but it was like being in the Arctic and we walked in all directions.

After six hours, we stopped for soup, drinking it quickly while slumped down on our sledges. We set off again just as the visibility improved. We were nearly through, and were coming to the ice-shelf proper, but the wind had died and it was only the power of our wasting muscles that could carry us on. I headed out. The last visible obstruction was past and there was just an empty horizon. I looked at the compass and set our heading for the next four hundred miles, aiming for a small cloud, a mark upon our bearing. Four hundred. Could we do it now? My legs felt fatigued beyond limits and since the soup stop they were somehow getting weaker. It was so, so cold, with a deep all-permeating chill. I felt detached from reality. My limbs were no longer my own, just heavy useless weights, and my mind floated freely from the shelf. Home, family, food, the three mainstays of my sanity wheeled before me, merging one with another in a haze of jumbled thought. I tried to concentrate, to look ahead and keep my course, but the horizon was a blur and with it my cloud kept moving. I began to meander, to slow, to stop.

'Mike . . . Mike!' Ran shouted at me. I heard him but it had no meaning. He told me later that I looked at him with puzzled, empty eyes, as if I were not in, and once more he had diagnosed hypothermia. It was an episode reminiscent of the one that occurred before the Pole, and again I must have been hypoglycaemic as well as cold. Yet on this occasion I had had no problem with my clothing and there was no vicious circle of events upon which to lay the blame. It seemed to be down to the sheer debilitation. I had lost nearly all my fatty insulation and was pitifully dressed for the conditions we faced. The day before, we had worked for fourteen (or was it fifteen?) hours to get to the Gate, and then we had eaten our meagre meal and worked late trying to produce new ski-sticks. After only a few hours of cold and restless sleep, we had gulped down our pathetic breakfast and were on our way once more. We had simply worked too hard and for too long for our rations and the cold. My blood glucose must have fallen and starved my brain of fuel, my core temperature dropped and my muscles just stopped working.

Ran put up the tent and gave me tea and chocolate. Gradually I recovered, remembering nothing. Unlike before, however, neither of us had the will to continue. The days where we could make up lost hours were gone. Down the Beardmore we had hurried, walking for twelve, thirteen, fourteen hours at a stretch, desperately seeking to take advantage of every minute of good weather. If it had closed in, we would have been slow and in danger – crevasses are a menace when visible; in mist they are impassable. Now we felt the cost of our efforts. It had had an obvious effect on me but Ran was affected too. His determination, that unquenchable fire which had carried us both across the wastes, was no longer what it had been. Exhaustion was dousing the flames that drove him on.

'Mike, after what happened today, I'm not sure that it's reasonable to continue. We were lucky it happened while you were leading. If you had slipped behind in the poor visibility, I could have lost you. There was no reason for it to happen this time. Perhaps we should be calling it a day.'

He was right. There had been no foolish under-dressing before this event. It would be best to give up. We had crossed the continent and were safe. It was stupid to go on into danger, particularly with only a small chance of success. But if we stopped now, it would for ever be my fault. No, I wasn't ready to be the cause. I would be happy if his foot flared up and we had to stop, but I didn't want to be our undoing.

'I know what you're saying,' I said, 'but I can't bear the thought of giving up when we have food and the possibility of making it remains. We've got fifteen half rations left, and

Messner took fourteen days from this point. I know he sailed the majority, but we might get that help too.'

'He didn't sail it all,' said Ran. 'He put in one or two days of big pulls. I'm not sure we can do it.'

'Well, you may be right, but I want one more chance. Another episode like today's and I promise that I'll throw in the towel, but not yet. Let's just see what we can still do.'

Because we had stopped early, we had longer in the tent than usual and took advantage of it to finish the ski-sticks we had been making. Up at the Gate, I had finally managed to cut the ski in half, and, by whipping ice screws to the bottom to act as baskets and weaving paracord handles, we made them function comfortably. Ran had spent a few evenings cutting empty fuel bottles to make metal baskets for the proper sticks and so, by the time we tried to sleep, we were back with a set each. A set of crutches might have been more useful.

Setting off the next day, I felt a bit better. We had had a longer rest than usual, and it was good to have a stick with a basket in each hand. We were better equipped than we had been for weeks and hauled along reasonably well in the cold sunshine. Yet, despite the rise in spirits, we knew that man-hauling was not the answer. We were too weak to go on for long without the wind. And we needed it soon.

All that day, and the following, it was bright, clear, cold, and very still. The surfaces were excellent and stronger men would have made good distance, but in the ten hours that was the most we could manage, we made only twelve miles. Despite sledges of half the weight with which we had started, we were moving at the same speed as when we had crossed the Filchner in the spring sunshine. We had never achieved that sixteen, seventeen miles per day. It was the end of the brief Antarctic summer, and although there were no leaves to fall to mark the turn of the seasons, it was becoming colder by the day. Even the hauling could no longer drive the chill from our bones. The cold lay heavily in our bodies and weakened us as effectively as venom. We had been crushed by the vastness of our journey, sapped by the weight of our loads, and now our muscles were poisoned by the ice.

If I was feeling it badly, Ran was feeling it more. With

my ankle easier on the flat, I could once again go much faster and it crushed his morale. The Beardmore had served to boost his self-confidence and he had forgotten much of the vision of his own mortality. Now he found it again, staring him in the face, and it was just as nasty as the first time. After my demoralising trip down the Beardmore, I did my best to avoid drawing too far ahead. The devastating effect of seeing one's partner striding away was fresh in my mind and I stopped and waited frequently rather than build any distance between us. Even then, I could not look back constantly, and once or twice his slowness caught me out. He could no longer bear the torment of his feet without reaction. The swelling on the right foot was now punctured by a deep hole, red, angry, inflamed with pus, and the black and swollen toes of both feet were demarcated by a vivid red line at the base where good tissue fought against the infection. The stench of rotting flesh was added to our already evil body odours.

On the third morning on the shelf, I set out at a fairly brisk pace, although no faster than the day before. Ran's feet were bad and I drew quite far ahead as a consequence of his pain. After some fifteen minutes I looked back to see where he was, and then stopped, standing in my traces waiting for him to come up. He was closer now and it suddenly struck me that it would make a beautiful picture. My sledge had carved a trail through the soft snow that lay on the shelf surface and the trail led back to Ran and on to the mountains beyond, lit by a low sun and glowing richly orange. I reached for my camera to preserve an image of history, and put it to my eye to compose and shoot. Before I could release the shutter I was amazed to see Ran suddenly deviate from the course and head off from the track. It immediately spoilt the picture, so I didn't take it, but I was curious as to what he might have seen, since I assumed there must be a reason for his suddenly going off line. I was wrong. He had seen nothing and simply walked in a large semi-circle that brought him back to me without stopping. When he arrived he was angry.

'Why did you set off so bloody fast?' he stormed, and there was accusation in his voice. 'You know my feet hurt and I can't keep up.'

'I didn't,' I replied. 'I went off at the same pace as always and just didn't realise that you weren't behind. Why did you walk off the track?'

'Ah, now there's a question,' he said enigmatically. 'I'm sure you know the answer.'

I was puzzled. Then it dawned on me – it was the camera. As we'd approached the Pole the aircraft that arrived to pick up the American women had flown out towards us. Ran had raced up from behind me to draw level, and it had been obvious that his concern was not to be photographed following rather than leading. Now it was the same again. He could handle a picture which showed him quite close, but was disturbed by the thought of a picture that showed him at any distance. It was another example of his leadership lark – even as we approached the end of this ordeal together, he had half a mind on the public relations of the weeks ahead. It made me fear for black dot stories, and of course, the Beardmore had given him a lot of ammunition. No, he wouldn't use it when for most of the expedition he had been behind. I had nothing to worry about.

I thought it prudent to avoid further discussion and just set off again, waited until I had got ahead and took the picture anyway. Whether it would have been any good I don't know. Like so many of our photographs, it was lost. The cold was too much for our cameras and their electronics, and despite keeping them inside our clothing, this was one of the many pictures that failed to materialise. In all, we had a disappointing photographic record of our trip.

We found that we couldn't see clearly. At first I thought that we must be suffering from the same blue light damage that Ran had sustained in the Arctic. There he had been unable to see anything sharply, whereas here it seemed more a question of focusing. Looking at the ground close by, I saw everything as sharp as a pin, but further away, towards the horizon, it was all very blurred. It was difficult to fix on far snow features and to stay on track. Neither of us could really see much beyond twenty feet. I wondered if it was our blood sugar. Perhaps we were constantly running low.

On the fourth day out on the shelf, the sun continued to

shine, and still there was no breath of wind. We began to feel demoralised. Each day without sailing made our chances of success grow slimmer. Now we had to have more luck than Messner in order to succeed. It also struck me for the first time that, if it did come to sailing, we would be extremely vulnerable. We could no longer defend our temperature when we were manhauling, so what would we be like when it was windy and we were not working so hard? If I could get hypothermic hauling on the shelf, then I could get hypothermic while using the up-ski. Then there was the frostbite. Ran's feet would almost immediately refreeze and my hands, where nine digits were now skinned down to the mid-point, could barely hold a spoon, let alone pull on cords and untangle knots. How many toes was it worth losing when our overall chance of success was all the time diminishing? How much more pain should we put ourselves through? I couldn't keep the thoughts to myself and discussed them with Ran in the tent that evening.

Again we concluded that, while there was still the possibility we would go on. But our discussion planted a seed in Ran's mind. On the fifth day out it grew, and was nurtured by the pain, the fatigue and the hunger. He came up at the soup stop almost shuffling – cold, tired and slow.

'Mike, it's no good. It's getting too cold and too dangerous. The mileage we're getting from the walking is hardly going to make any difference. Let's shorten our day, eat more frequently and be more realistic about our chances. If, in the next few days, we get wind, we will use it for as many hours as it will give us, but it's only sailing that can make a difference, not the walking.'

What he said was welcome in some ways but not in others, and it was not entirely true. Even moving slowly we were covering more than ten miles a day, so there was a good hundred miles to be had even without wind, and any sailing could add to that. Mind you, if we knocked only a couple of hours off each day it would cost only about twenty miles. I supposed that wouldn't make much difference.

'What exactly do you propose?' I said.

'I think we should put all our hours back to normal length

165

and just do eight hours for a day or two. Honestly, we just can't go on in this cold with so little food.'

'Well, I suppose you are right. But there is just one other thing we could do.'

'What's that?' Ran asked.

I was hesitant. I didn't know if I really wanted to put any counter arguments. So much of me either wanted out, or at least a decrease in our hours. As before, I wanted nothing more than to stop, but when the possibility arose, I wanted to go on.

'It might be worth switching our day by twelve hours and moving into the local daytime,' I said. 'It probably won't be much warmer, but it could be enough to make a difference.'

I didn't know what effect this might have. We were still endeavouring to travel with the sun behind us. Since it was local night, we might be making our travelling time colder for ourselves than need be. Although the sun didn't dip below the horizon, it did dip significantly at night, and although we would have the sun in our eyes, daytime travel might be warm enough to keep going.

'Well, we can talk about that in the tent,' Ran said. 'Personally I don't think it will make a ha'porth of difference, but in any case let's shorten today and do straight hours for the remainder.'

'That's fine by me,' I replied.

When we set off again, I felt frustrated. Even though I had said the night before that things were bad, now that Ran was being negative I didn't want to hear it. I needed to press on until I was sure we could go no further, but as previously in the expedition, I needed Ran to make sure that I didn't give up. We went on for only an hour more before Ran stopped and turned to me again.

'It wasn't what I wanted to say,' he started. 'It came out all wrong. I think we should stop and put up the tent and talk about where we can go from here. Then, if you want to go on, this evening we can switch into the day time phase as you suggested.'

So this was it. I was surprised. He was obviously going to suggest stopping altogether. I had been waiting for the moment for so long and now it was here I definitely didn't want it. It was astonishing to hear this coming from him. Even though I had been saying something like it the night before, it had been thoughts rather than hard proposals. I never believed that I would hear Ran suggesting that we should stop while there was still an outside chance of success. At least, not independent of an incident like the hypothermia a few days before.

We said little while we erected the tent and made tea. After that it was a long time before either of us would broach the subject. I was waiting for Ran to start and I think he was hesitant because he felt unsure of my response. Finally he began.

'I've never been the one to step back from difficult decisions,' he announced. 'Now we have to consider our options seriously. If we go on, we may achieve overall success but it's looking increasingly unlikely. We have to examine what we have achieved and what risks there are if we don't stop now.'

I merely nodded and waited. I knew what he was going to say, but I needed to hear it from him. Then I had to think about it. My immediate reaction was still to say no, we mustn't stop, not now, after all this time. There was still a chance. We must go on trying. Yet, at the same time, I knew my own weaknesses. Without his determination I would have stopped before this and, if we were going to fail, we might as well do it quickly.

After a long pause I said, 'Go on.'

'We have already achieved most of what we set out to do.' Ran continued. 'We've crossed the continent, made the longest unsupported journey ever, will have raised millions for charity, and your scientific programme is a success.' He paused. 'All we haven't achieved is to cross the ice-shelf, the ice-shelf that isn't part of the continent. We have only seen it as part for romantic reasons. We had to cross it when there was still a chance of catching our ship, but that sails in five days' time and there's no possibility of reaching it before then. To go on would be to take real risks, and it would only be for the Polar pundits and our own satisfaction. We know from Mo's messages that our journey has already been accepted as a success, and the longer we leave it before we go back, the less impact our return will make from a PR point of view. We are in danger. You said yourself last night that we would probably get frostbite and hypothermia if we sailed, and I am sure you're right. Half a degree warmer, gained by travelling in the daytime isn't going to make any difference. We'll still be too cold, and we'll still run the risks. Look at your hands and my feet.'

He held them up and I saw the blackened toes with an evil red margin, and I looked at the insides of my fingers, poking bare and sore through the remnants of blackened skin.

'They could blow up at any time, you said it yourself, and we've run out of antibiotics and anti-inflammatories. The season is getting on, the weather could close us down, and if we don't make Scott Base we could find ourselves out on the ice-shelf with no food in a storm that blows for a week. We could quite easily end up doing a Scott, you know. I think that it's just too risky to go on.'

For a minute or two neither of us spoke. We sat in silence and sipped our tea. Everything he said was correct, but did it really have to come to this? To the vast majority of people who had heard that we had crossed the Antarctic, going on to finish the ice-shelf would seem pointless, but we were not the vast majority of people. We knew in our hearts, or at least I did in mine, that we had not completed what we set out to do. For me it would probably be difficult to live with, and much more so since a possibility remained that it was still achievable. It would be so much easier if we tried and failed. But he was right about our vulnerabilities. If his foot became infected now, as it constantly threatened to do, we didn't have the treatment to deal with it. He could succumb to septicaemia in hours, and it could kill him even if an aircraft were to come promptly. We could get cold, particularly if sailing, and in a wind and poor visibility we might become separated and one of us could be lost. We could have that combination of storm and radio blackout that would see us stuck with no food for days or even weeks. Yes, we could do a Scott. We could do it quite easily.

'What you say is right,' I said, 'but I don't want to agree with you. We will both live with the disappointment if we don't make it all the way, especially when there's an outside chance that we might have been able to.'

'No ... Not me ... I won't,' he said immediately. 'What we've done together is a fantastic achievement and everyone will see it so. I'm quite happy with it. It's way beyond what we anticipated, and we have crossed the continent. We have made the longest unsupported journey ever. Listen. I'll go on for as long as you want to, and we can switch to the day to see if it helps, but I don't think it's worth the risk and we will not make it.'

I didn't know what to say. We had been out and going for more than three months and I craved to go home. I craved the safety and my family and the food. Above all, I craved the end of the work, the toil, the dreadful exhaustion. But if we gave up now, how would I feel in the future? I suppose it might depend on whether we were met by congratulations or commiserations. I certainly couldn't bear another episode like the North Pole when we broke all records, raised millions and were greeted by a hail of bad lucks. It had been inevitable but crushing. At the same time, whatever I felt like doing, I also had to be realistic. If I said 'no' now, we would carry on, but it wouldn't last. The next day when we started hauling and the cold, the pain, and the fatigue sought us out again, I knew that I would turn to Ran and say 'Okay, let's stop.' It wasn't in me to drive us on; it never had been and I was sure it was not there now. I knew myself well enough for that. I needed Ran's volition in order to carry on. He had given me my out, it was no longer my fault if we were to stop.

'Okay ...' I said slowly, 'Let's call in the plane and get out of here. We've done the best we can.'

There, I had said it, and it was all over. All the pain, all the suffering was finishing. Ran smiled, I did too.

'No, not the best we can,' he said. 'Don't view it like that. Never be negative about it or it will consume you. We have done it. We completed our journey five days ago when we went through the Gate. It's been a journey that will probably never be equalled. Even if it is repeated, we led the way. We did it first.'

Ran reached for the radio and I went outside for a moment.

The little tent stood in the middle of the white plain with the sun shining on it. It felt quite warm on my face, but the air was cold. To the west there were the mountains and they ran away to the north, to that point where the ice-shelf finished and Scott Base stood by the open water. To the south, they disappeared over the horizon, accompanied by a thin dark line that ran backwards from our tent. Beyond that horizon, the line went on, back to Mount Hope, where it turned, through the Gate and then up the glacier, and across crevasses, the blue-ice, and the wind-filled valleys. It crossed the ice weir to the high plateau and then ran due south to the Pole. It went on further – straight for another few hundred miles, and then more tortuously as it dropped down through valleys, dunes and sastrugi to meet the ice-shelf on the other side, the mirror of where I stood. Finally it ran across that shelf, and passed Berkner Island to reach Gould Bay where a snow petrel had fluttered. It was the longest, unbroken track that a man had ever made.

EPILOGUE

★

Also Ran

WITH THE RELEASE from the expedition came release from our self-imposed starvation. In the three hours after stopping I ate twelve chocolate bars, consumed two main meals and drank tea continuously.

The aircraft picked us up swiftly and whisked us from the middle of nowhere back to Patriot Hills. There everything had changed. The busy base that we had last seen three months earlier was now dismantled. Almost nothing remained except one tent, although when you entered you realised that it was not a tent at all. It was the entrance to an underground snow cave, dug by hand and taking weeks of labour. It contained a single-engine Cessna aircraft and a vast array of stores to be left in the Antarctic for the winter. Beside it, also sheltered from the ravages of the wind, there was a small living quarter occupied by the crews of the two Twin Otters who had waited in Antarctica for our final call. They were eager to get out before the winter closed in, for they too had been away from their families for the entire southern summer. With the weather getting more risky by the minute, the sooner they got themselves and their aircraft off the continent the better.

With our return to Patriot Hills Ran and I were transformed from function to decrepitude. Just a few hours before, we had been pulling our loads across the ice-fields; now we collapsed. After the last halt, and the decision to stop, it was as if something snapped. Our determination, the will that had driven us was gone, and with it went all strength and we were reduced to a state of helplessness hardly to be imagined. While the air crews were busy with their final clear up, dismantling the radio

SHADOWS ON THE WASTELAND

aerials and loading the last items aboard the planes, Ran and I lay in the dark snow cave barely able to get to our feet. Even eating – a drive that was overwhelming from a mental point of view – was a physical struggle, and going to the lavatory took a supreme effort of will. Walking had become almost impossible. Without the pumping action in our legs that had been achieved by our rhythmic motion for ten hours a day, the fluid of our circulation now seeped through the walls of damaged blood vessels. Normally these would have been repaired by the body, but, due to starvation, the repair systems had broken down. We had been consuming ourselves as we walked, burning the boat to fuel the engine, and with no materials to spare, the blood vessels leaked into the surrounding tissues and our legs swelled grotesquely as if we had elephantiasis. With our weakened muscles and the weight of these swollen limbs, we were virtually bedridden. We finally needed help to get aboard the aircraft.

The thirty-hour journey back to Chile was a torment that neither of us would ever wish to repeat. The little aircraft bucked and swung in the turbulent air above the peninsular mountains. In the hot rear cabin, perched on tiny canvas seats and wedged between a full cargo and additional barrels of fuel, we felt as sick as dogs. To be so hungry yet so nauseated was an unwelcome combination, and the journey was relieved only when we made an enforced call at the British Antarctic Survey base of Rothera. This was necessitated by the discovery that the majority of the ice landing strip in Jones Sound had broken out. It was used by ANI as a fuel dump, but when the pilot landed on the grossly foreshortened runway, he feared that with a full load he would never be able to get off again. The only thing he could do was to relay barrels of fuel and ourselves the few miles down the coast to Rothera, and then stash everything on the runway before going back empty for more. After a couple of trips he should be able to get enough fuel to Rothera for fully laden take-off and the crossing of Drake Passage. We were about to fly one of the most hostile oceans in the world in a small aircraft that needed to be refuelled in the air by the co-pilot hand-pumping a barrel on the seat next to me.

At Rothera we had a wonderful reception and spent a

couple of hours chatting to the base staff and looking round. With our sickness diminishing, we began to eat ravenously – toast and eggs, then soup and bread, and then more toast and eggs, and then just toast. We were both surprised to find that we still couldn't see properly. Sitting in the large dining room, I was unable to focus on anything more than a few yards away. Across the room, the notice board was an unreadable blur and the mountains outside were hazy. I couldn't understand it. With recently emptied plates, there was no possibility that we could still be hypoglycaemic.

Back in Britain, the mystery was to be explained. It had been known for decades that, with nothing to look at, the eye will focus at about one metre in front of it, and this effect had been implicated in a number of aircraft accidents. Pilots looking out through the window into a cloudless sky become accommodated and focused on a point shortly in front of their face without realising that they can no longer see clearly at a distance. When another aircraft appears in front of them, they take no evasive action to avoid a mid-air collision. Of course, pilots turn and look round their cockpits every few moments and land at an airport within a few hours. We had spent weeks looking at precisely nothing, and now our eyes had become so used to fixing on that near point that they had lost the ability to do much else. The muscles that controlled the focusing system had become weak with disuse and it would be a fortnight before we could see again properly. It was the first time that anything like it had been reported in the annals of ophthalmology, and my guess is that there won't be many similar reports in the future.

It took ten days in all to reach England – ten days of exhaustion and illness mixed with excitement and mental euphoria. Once home, the full measure of our physical debilitation was documented, and our scientific tests confirmed the appalling state to which we had been reduced. I had gone from being a strong individual to someone who by any standards was weak. My leg muscles had lost 60 per cent of their strength and now had the power of the elderly or frail. This was clearly visible to the naked eye, but things were worse than they appeared. Another savagely painful biopsy revealed the hidden magnitude of our self-destruction. Not only were the muscles small, they were internally useless. The levels of the proteins in them – the enzymes that provided the powerhouse of their structure – had fallen dramatically. With the prolonged exercise, one would have expected the levels to rise, but we had consumed the contents of our cells and there was little left to provide the force of contraction.

There were also some strange changes in our metabolism – the rate at which the body ticks over and uses fuel. When people go on diets to lose weight, they generally find that after a few weeks the diet is no longer effective. This is largely due to a drop in the resting metabolic rate as the body does its best to compensate for the food shortage. It is well known that this effect can be offset to an extent by exercise, and that if you combine dieting with exercise, the efficiency of a diet can continue for much longer. We had taken this to extremes. While eating what by normal standards would be deemed excessive, we had lost weight by exercising continually. Our resting metabolism had gone sky high, but quite why this change occurred is beyond me. As an adaptation, it was enormously wasteful, burning more energy than was necessary.

Our hunger came home with us. The KLM staff could scarcely credit the quantities we put away in the eighteen hours of flight back from South America. They gave up bringing us individual extra portions when we asked and took to giving us complete extra meal trays. Back in England, it continued; the drive could not be ignored. We ate all day, filling ourselves to the point of continuous discomfort and then were eating again as soon as there was any room. I even ate at night, waking ravenous and struggling downstairs on swollen and frostbitten feet to raid the fridge. It was the only way to get back to sleep.

During this time, we completed our studies of protein turnover to see what happened after the journey had ended. It meant collecting more urine samples while keeping a record of what we ate. Now I look back in amazement at those records, with Ran recording a breakfast of muesli, sugar puffs, toast, and eggs at 8 a.m. and then five jam doughnuts with coffee an hour later, with the rest of the day going on in the same vein.

174

Even after a week or two of eating, our weakness persisted.
I found that I couldn't walk upstairs without holding on to the
banisters and pulling with my arms, and I couldn't get up from
a chair without difficulty. My children seemed so much heavier
than before I had left, and even the three-year-old Tarn was too
heavy for me to carry any distance. I had dreamed of being their
horse up to bed, but it was I who needed carrying, and when
it came to building that Wendy house, I went out and bought
one. I just couldn't face it. I did none of those jobs around the
house and the car was left resolutely in the garage.

There was no doubt that we were in a sorry state, certainly
weaker and more vulnerable than I had realised at the time of
our stopping. Yet, despite feeling so weak, and all the measurements supporting the wisdom of pulling out when we did,
I remained unhappy with the outcome without knowing quite
why. Although sometimes what we had achieved would strike
home, and I would suddenly see all those miles in their vast
perspective, for much of the time I felt depressed about our
achievement. I couldn't even complain when we got back to
England that there was anything but praise. The press had a
field day and we received the ultimate accolade of appearing in
many newspaper cartoons. We were feted as national heroes.
Even respected experts rated our feat highly, and men such
as Chris Bonnington drew parallels with the first ascent of
Everest. Many children from schools all over Britain sent us
congratulations cards, as did many multiple sclerosis sufferers
who also sent their thanks. The Prime Minister wrote with
generous congratulations. We were applauded on all sides for
what we had done, and the fact that we had not crossed my
finishing line meant nothing to anyone but me. If only I had
insisted on going on, perhaps we would have made it, or at
least have reached the position where I knew there was no other
option but to stop and call for pick-up. I recognise that to go
on would have been at considerable risk, but I cannot escape
the conclusion that we copped out. Part of my mind goes on
telling me that 'after all that time, effort and pain, in the end
you couldn't stick it'.

There is one aspect of this self doubt that does please me.
Before I went on the trip I had questioned whether I did it

for the challenge and my own sense of achievement or for the recognition and glory. Now I have the answer. Yes, I enjoyed the public acclaim, but that alone was not enough. Praise for the achievement of our journey went beyond my wildest dreams, but I was not satisfied. It mattered to me that I had not reached the summit of this 'Snowdon' I had chosen to climb. The fact that I cared more about that than what others thought proved to me that it was a very personal challenge.

What does Ran think of the expedition in retrospect? I am not altogether sure, but he also has some problems with where we stopped, and has gone through some soul searching as to whether we could have made it to the end. Certainly he remembers the bad times better than I, and Ginny has told me that he hardly talks of the journey, even to her or to close friends. He can remember the endless pain in his foot, the nightmare of fatigue, and the recognition of his own frailty. It is probably the last that hurts him the most, and that spoils everything for him. He said it on the trip, and he said it after the end. Although what he did was really an enormous achievement, an absolute triumph for a man of his age, I fear he will remember it as the trip too far. Nevertheless he hints at things to come.

What of our relationship after the expedition? When eventually we finished we were on good terms. What we had endured together had forged a comradeship that was strong enough to bear the difficulties that tried to tear us apart. We could both be harsh, yet we had also shown our capacity for tolerance. Few people could have been through what we had together and done better.

After our return to England I saw the old attitudes and public face swiftly cover it all up. Why couldn't I laugh when the familiar black dot stories reappeared? As the small deviations from fact grew in number, so I became intensely irritated with Ran. I knew him as well as any man can know another, and accepted that what I saw as his foibles were merely masks over his strength, yet I found myself resenting the press interviews in which Ran always qualified his confession that he had become angry when I led too fast with the comment that when he was leading I couldn't keep up. Why couldn't he say that this was the case only when I was struggling downhill on the Beardmore Glacier with a broken ankle? How dare he say, when admitting that his age had finally caught up with him, that I was really too small to be good at pulling those loads? The diarrhoea episode became unrecognisable. Instead of speaking of his frustration with my illness, I read that I had wanted to stop but he had forced me on. He had had to 'exert his leadership', he told the newspapers, and had found that 'being leader, you could not always be popular'. It made me spit. The incident had more in common with a reversion to childhood.

Beardmore black dot stories were also popular. Ran had been wonderful to let me have one of his ski-sticks after I lost mine, and there had been that episode when, for an hour, he had let me have both sticks. Now it seemed that I had both for virtually the entire length of the glacier. My being happy for him to stay out in front because of my ankle making me slow, and his getting cold, now became his leading on the Beardmore because of his skill. My being out in front elsewhere was changed from 'leading' to 'scouting', a new term that he invented at the end of the expedition. It was the verbal equivalent of not wanting photographs showing him behind. It was all so unnecessary and trivial when compared with the depth of friendship that in reality had pulled us through.

Yet, although these corruptions annoy me, I don't believe they are malicious. Ran has always exaggerated and will naturally embellish an event to make a good story. He is a consummate master at public relations and he knows what people want to hear. Hardship and heroism, struggle and strife, they must all be hyped up a bit for public consumption, and so the subtle alterations come about almost subconsciously, and then slowly evolve. Finally they alter the whole beyond recognition, and once told a couple of times, the stories become his reality. Indeed, when I pointed out the discrepancies, Ran was genuinely surprised. I don't think he ever deliberately did me down, and my anger is tempered by this belief.

There is one last and difficult question. Everyone I speak to, almost invariably ends up asking me if I would do it, or something like it, again. The answer is that I would. Even though I can clearly remember saying to myself every day of the journey 'I must never do this again', I don't feel now as I did then. The memory deficit is playing its tricks already and a restlessness is beckoning. I can see challenges waiting to be met, most of them probably impossible, but so was our unsupported crossing of Antarctica before we did it. If I were given the chance, I would go back tomorrow to repeat the journey and finish what was left undone.

When I express such sentiments today, they are often met with more of those looks of incomprehension – as if I were crazy. I can only say there are those things that last when all else is forgotten. In the Antarctic I saw my life in a different perspective. I conducted my science and learned a great deal, and I supported a worthy cause and raised a lot of money for it. Most of all, I took up a challenge and, despite frequently wanting to give up, pushed myself hard. Perhaps it is true that I am a few stock cubes short of a ration, but if that is so, I can't say I'm troubled by it.

It will not happen again soon, not least for the commitment I must make to my family. But, if the opportunity were to come again to step out of life and visit other planets, there is no question as to whom I would wish for a companion. I would go with Ran.

I would like to thank all the sponsors who made our expeditions possible and all those working with the Multiple Sclerosis Society who made them more worthwhile.

M.S. June 1993

from *The Spectator*

TRANS-ANTARCTIC EXPEDITION

Equipment and Supplies

	Number	Weight (lbs)
Sledge	two	52
Harness/traces	two	7
Skis (pairs)	two	18
Spare ski and binding	one	4.5
Skins (pairs)	four	4
Skin glue	two	2
Ski sticks (pairs)	two	5
Tent	one	12
Spare tent poles	two	1
Snow stakes	six	1.5
Tent brush	one	0.5
Stove and box (pans/mugs)	one	9.5
Spare stove and pan	one	1.5
Thermoses (full)	two	16
Sleeping bags (double)	two	27
Sleeping mats	four	8
HF radio	one	13
Radio batteries	two	4
Personal Locator Beacons	two	2
PLB batteries	four	1.5
Magellan GPS	two	6
Sarsat Beacon	one	8
Sarsat batteries	two	2
Scientific kit	one	10
Cameras	two	3.5
Video kit	one	8
Medical kit	one	4

	Number	Weight (lbs)
Repairs kit	one	1.5
Ice axe	one	2
Ice screws	two	0.5
Jumars (pairs)	two	2
Snow shovel	one	0.5
Rope	one	6.5
Sledge compass	one	2
Rucksacks	two	9
Windsails	two	23
Spare clothing/knife diary/film/etc.	two	26
Rations (2 man)	101	510
Fuel (1 litre)	66	144

Total weight of clothing, equipment and supplies amounted to 485 lbs per man

Clothing

Worn clothing:
Plastic double boots
Over-gaiters
Socks (inner, vapour
    barrier and outer)
Longjohns
Long-sleeve undertop
Fibre pile salopettes
Fleece jacket with
    windproofing
Goretex overtrousers
Ventile sledging jacket
Inner gloves
Goretex/pile outer mitts
Balaclava
Windproof headband
Goggles/sunglasses

Spare clothing:
Inner gloves
Dachstein woollen mitts
Windproof mitts
Balaclava
Sunglasses
Inner socks
Outer socks

Bibliography

Apsley Cherry-Gerrard, *The Worst Journey in the World*, Constable, London, 1922

T. S. Eliot, *The Waste Land*, Faber & Faber, London, 1925

Sir Ranulph Fiennes, *To the Ends of the Earth: Transglobe Expedition 1979-82*, Hodder and Stoughton, London, 1983

——, *Atlantis of the Sands*, Bloomsbury, London, 1992

Sir Vivian Fuchs and Sir Edmund Hillary, *The Crossing of the Antarctic*, Cassell, London, 1958

Wally Herbert, *Across the Top of the World: The British Trans-Arctic Expedition*, Longmans, London, 1969

——, *The North Pole*, Sackett and Marshall, London, 1979

Reinhold Messner, *Antarctica, Both Heaven and Hell*, Crowood Press, Marlborough, 1991

Reader's Digest, *Antarctica*, Reader's Digest Services Pty Ltd, NSW, 1985

Captain R. F. Scott, *Scott's Last Expedition*, Smith, Elder, London, 1913

Sit Ernest Shackleton, *South: The Story of Shackleton's Last Expedition*, Heinemann, London, 1919

Robert Swan and Roger Mear, *In the Footsteps of Scott*, Jonathan Cape, London, 1987